ROCK AND ROLL MELTDOWN
The Circus Nightclub Story, 1979-1983

By
Rick Bandazian

First published by Dog Ear Publishing
4010 W. 86th Street, Ste H
Indianapolis, IN 46268
www.dogearpublishing.net

ISBN: 978-1-4575-3208-5

Library of Congress Control Number: has been applied for

This book is printed on acid-free paper.

Printed in the United States of America

INTRODUCTION

I never knew how difficult it would be to write a book until I started writing. At first it came easily. The events, memories, times, and places were a snap to recollect and reduce to writing. But with only 10 short chapters on paper, it became more and more difficult to find the words that would deliver true expression and the factual data necessary for you, the reader, to relive a special time in rock and roll history. Our time! Our era! New Jersey style!

I toyed with the idea of bringing in a ghostwriter but quickly knew that it wouldn't work for me. Sports celebrities, movie stars, politicians, and everyday people with big bucks do it all the time. I'm not knocking it; it's just not for me. After all, how could I expect someone else to pretend they knew what it was like to have lived in a specific time and place? Would a ghostwriter really know what it was like to have a dance floor shaking under their feet in a rock club or feel the power and sound of floor-to-ceiling Marshall amps sending a chill through your young body, night after night? Would they know what it was like to be in a band back in the day, playing their hearts out five and six nights a week, reaching for stardom that seldom came? Would they know what it was like to work at or own a rock club in the late 70s and early 80s?

This book describes this fallen rock scene, a time that will live forever in the hearts of those who were there and can truly appreciate the magic. There are up-close and personal interviews from real people, including former and current band members of some of the greatest original, cover, and tribute bands to ever rock the club scene. You'll be captivated by interviews from then-kids, who went from rock club to rock club seeking great music five or six nights a week and their eye witness accounts of what it was really like. Also, interviews with former employees from back in the day tell their story, a story that can only be told through their eyes.

The experience of writing this book was more rewarding than I ever imagined. I had the privilege and fortune to reconnect with so many great people and found that there's one common thread that connects us all. Like a club or a fraternity, we're all a special group of people that feel the electricity when we speak about our era, the club scene, and the fact that we all lived it. We sparkle when we reminisce about it. If you were there, you know what I mean.

DEDICATION

This book is dedicated to my dad, Jack Bandazian, Sr. who passed away during the production of this book. I regret that he didn't get to see and read the finished product. Without you, there wouldn't have been a book or a story to tell. You had the guts to go 'all in' when we opened Circus-Circus back in 1979. After running three successful businesses with me, you rolled the dice again and never looked back. When things were going to shit, you never complained or whimpered. Thanks for taking the shot with me and Jack Jr. Even though we walked away with only the shirts on our backs, who would have known 35 years later that you would be a small part of rock and roll history from that very special era. There were lots of memories, some good and others not so good. But overall, you'd have to say, we had a good run!

TABLE OF CONTENTS

PREFACE

Before I start boring you with the "thank yous" and the "without so-and-so this book could not have been possible" crap, let me tell you some facts. Everything I write is the truth to the best of my recollection, including details such as events, dates, and times, which countless hours of research will attest. Still, there may be errors and omissions, so I'll apologize for that in advance.

There are so many great bands and solo artists that are not mentioned in this book or barely mentioned, but I thank you for contributing to the era and particularly our club, Circus-Circus, later The Circus. I would also like to thank all rock clubs wherever they are or were in America, and around the world. You were and still are the rock and roll heroes of our generation.

About the name Circus-Circus; let me be clear. We never, ever had any affiliation or association with Circus Circus Hotels, Inc., Circus Circus Hotel and Casino in Las Vegas, or any of their affiliates. The reason we changed the name to The Circus on or about January 1, 1981 was to avoid potential litigation. They didn't like us using their name. Can you blame them? Representatives for Circus Circus Hotels, Inc. were kind and gave us reasonable time to change our trade name, signs, marketing, and so on. Tell you about that later.

ACKNOWLEDGEMENTS

TO MY BROTHER JACK

Without you, we wouldn't have been a rock club. You had the vision, persistence, and a knack for hiring talent. Without you, we would've been another restaurant or bar serving up scungilli and fried calamari. Mangia!

It's hard to imagine a 20-year-old kid today having the kind of responsibility that you had, booking great bands and solo artists and dealing with some pretty seasoned sharks in the business.

I couldn't have asked for a better partner.

We weren't the biggest or the smallest club, but you had the deep-seated belief that we were THE BEST, and that's precisely what attracted every great band to South Washington Avenue in Bergenfield, New Jersey.

When you told me you could book The Police for $5,000 I remember saying, "Who's the Police?" I thought they were empowered by the government to enforce the law. I knew then that I needed a crash course on ROCK and ROLL.... Thanks for the on-the-job training!

When you booked Rick Danko from the legendary rock group The Band, I didn't have a clue who he was either, but when he played The Circus, the fans knew. They probably also knew that The Band would one day wind up in the Rock and Roll Hall of Fame. I only found out recently that Rick did a world tour in 1966 with Bob Dylan. He could play 10 different instruments, masterfully. Lots of history there! In 1983 you booked Steve Forbert, best known for Romeo's Tune. He's an amazing artist and still rocking it today.

Then there was Robert Hunter, lyricist for the Grateful Dead and early friend of Jerry Garcia, who played The Circus in 1982. Robert was an early research test subject for psychedelic chemicals at Stanford University, covertly sponsored by the CIA. According to Wikipedia, he was paid to take LSD, psilocybin, and mescaline and report on his experience.

Where am I going with all this? I don't know. But you can't make this stuff up!

TO MY SISTER AND BEST FRIEND DIANE GUTHRIE

Thank you for your support, loyalty, unconditional love, confidence, and encouragement. You've always been my rock through thick and thin.

THOSE WHO OFFERED THEIR TIME AND MEMORIES

Donald Labe; Darren Prince; Harry Sweeney; Maureen and Tom Crispino; Mary Beth O'Hara; Ricky Pops; Tom Corea; Joe Dolan; Jay Dittamo; Marc Muller; Billy Mueller; Carl C.J. Mueller; Donny Mueller; Mark and George Lefkandinos; Bo Blaze; Johnny Sing; Steve Scerenscko; Keith McElwee; Robert (Coconut) Doudoukjian; Bob Dynan; Douglas Carter; Lenny Molinari; Bill Hicks; Ed Piersanti; Rich Gulya; JJ French; Liz Dobler; Richard Verge; Jay O'Buck; Bill Sasse; Chris Madden; Dan Muro; Vinnie Lanza; Don Siudmak; Mark Tornillo; Dan Wos; Jim Garcia; Cliff Witmyer; Eugene Introna; Paul Censullo; Andrew Politi; Mark Dicarlo; Kit and Lou Tedesco; Frank White; Jim Mason; George Erlich; Donna Rheaume; Renee Bandazian; Nora Curran; Ross Dodwell; Danny Dooner; Gil Gallego; Billy Schorling; Bryant Lutz; Dirk Vuijst; Joe and Linda Wolfson, Bruce Fishon.

I'd like to acknowledge the editorial contributions made by Eddie Riveria from Los Angeles, California.

Special thanks to Dan Lorenzo for locating, conducting, and writing some very revealing interviews with band members and others.

LEGAL

Barry A. Cohen, Law Firm of Gelman and Gelman, New Jersey. Thanks for keeping us out of trouble....well, sometimes!

I still remember bartending at a private party in your home. It helped me earn some extra bucks while we were waiting to open the club.

And, how can I forget the closing when we sold our diner and a dispute arose causing the buyer's attorney to threaten my father that he would throw him out the window if we didn't settle it quickly. I think he was in a rush to get home! RIP Barry!

ACCOUNTING

George Kalosieh, partner in the accounting firm of Edelman and Kalosieh, New Jersey.

I was always impressed with the speed at which you ran the numbers on your calculator. One hundred miles an hour wouldn't be exaggerating. I think some of it rubbed off on Joe!

Joe Shackil, formally with Edelman and Kalosieh. Now Kalosieh, Shackil, & Meola, CPAs PA, New Jersey.

On the first of every month, Joe and I would meet at Circus-Circus to do the books. Joe was in his 20s like the rest of us, and you could just tell he liked his monthly visit to the club. Thanks for keeping us out of trouble with Uncle Sam.

TECHNICAL SUPPORT

Special thanks to Mark Scala and Symmetre Design Group, Ridgewood, New Jersey, for their support through cyberspace and Mark's creative talent in creating and designing the jacket cover for this book.

PRE CIRCUS-CIRCUS

It would probably be more interesting if I said I grew up in "the hood," but that wouldn't be true. The town of Glen Rock, New Jersey was far from it, but not geographically or socioeconomically. Glen Rock was a quiet bedroom community with great schools, a train station, and enough friends on your street to have a kickball game every day of the week until the street lights came on. At just 11 years old we jumped on buses and headed to the city or the Garden State Plaza in Paramus, New Jersey—the mall of malls back then—without a worry in the world. Even if it was dangerous to hang out unchaperoned at our young age, we didn't know it. Even better, our parents didn't know it.

We'd go bowling, to the movies, roller skating at the rink, and I don't recall anyone checking up on us. Everywhere felt safe.

When I was 13, I got a job at the luncheonette down the street from my house. My job was to insert the different sections into each newspaper every Saturday and Sunday morning.

I started at 6 am. The pay was good–50¢ an hour, and I thought I was going to be rich. Bob and Joe owned the place, and as time went by Joe became like a second father to me. I really loved the man.

One time, three of my friends and I cut school, and Joe let us hide in the store's basement. We played cards, shared a beer, and smoked cigarettes. Joe even sent down the waitress to take our lunch order. All my friends thought he was cool. We got busted that very day for cutting school, but no one ratted on Joe. You just didn't do that.

After I'd worked at the store for about a month, the counter help didn't show up. I was the fill-in guy that day. I quickly learned how to cook, make ice cream sundaes, and serve everything on the menu. In the summer, I worked almost every day and took as many hours as I could get. I got a raise to 75¢ an hour and then to a buck an hour. I got the taste for money at a young age and learned the value of saving what I earned.

When I was sixteen, I convinced my father to open a place of our own in South Hackensack, New Jersey. Our place was a combination luncheonette/sweetshop/stationery store, located right next to a barbershop, which the landlord owned. We kept the place open until 10 PM every night in hopes of turning a profit. Still too young to drive, my mother would pick me up from school and drive me to the store. Then, at closing time, either my father or mother would come back for me.

One dark October night, I remember three guys pulling up directly in front of the store. One got out of the car and began walking toward my front door. It was about 9:30 PM or so, and it was rare seeing a customer at this late hour. "Suspicious Guy" walked in and began eyeballing the store corner to corner. He looked at me and also looked to see if anyone else was behind the counter, but all he saw was this skinny kid—me.

There was just no one around, on the streets or anywhere, and the parking lot seemed to get darker and darker as I looked outside hoping someone else would pull in. Then I noticed the car they came in was no longer in the same parked position. It was now backed into the spot facing busy Huyler Street. Being streetwise, I knew that they were casing the place, and I was seconds or minutes away from being robbed.

Now, I'm thinking as my heart pounds: Did I have enough money in the cash register to satisfy them? Would they kill me? Did he have a knife or a gun? As the adrenaline raced in my veins, we both looked outside at the same time and saw the headlights of another car pulling into the lot.

Come in! Come in! Please come in, I thought to myself. I could easily have been saying that out loud. My heart was pounding out of my chest, and I was sure he could hear that, too.

It was as though a guardian angel was looking over me. The car wasn't just any car. It was a South Hackensack police cruiser. Suspicious Guy quickly walked out when he saw the cop stroll toward my door. The Guy and his band, "The Suspicious Buddies," quickly left the parking lot. From the moment the cop pulled up, everything seemed to speed up, and the next thing I knew, the store was empty again. Still shaking from the experience, I explained to the officer what had just happened. The cop never got the cigarettes he intended to buy. I'd sold the last pack of Lucky Strikes the day before and was waiting for a delivery. His need for a smoke might have saved my young life.

I quickly learned that South Hackensack was no Glen Rock. Just weeks later, another frightening experience took place, as if we weren't already ready to make tracks out of there. Everyone called him "Hot Dog Joe." He would set up his Sabrett hot dog cart every day in front of the two-family house next to our store, where he and his wife lived. I could see Joe and his busy pushcart world just by gazing out the side window of our place.

It was maybe 4 pm on a Friday. Out of the long, quiet afternoon, I heard the screeching of a car's tires. Almost at the same time, there's this crazy commotion going in "Joe Town." From the window, I saw Joe ditch his cart and sprint into the house, as if chased by his own ghost. That alone was a small miracle. Joe was legally blind.

Then came Joe's wife clambering out of her car with a shiny blue-steel shotgun—the scariest thing I'd ever seen. Hell, I'd never seen a gun of any kind in a public place, let alone right over there, in front of me!

"Wifey is off the rails now."

"You cheating bastard!" she yelled, and she open-fired on the second floor. I didn't know what to do. I'm stuck to my spot at the window. Okay, I'm thinking. There's a pay phone that we use, and it's, oh, right in the line of fire. Hmm.

In her state, she could have easily fired off a round at my head if she saw me trying to call for help. I tried to leave the store and get into the barbershop to have someone call the police, but as I moved toward the front door, I realized I was strolling back into firing range again. Wifey had the whole street at bay.

I quickly ducked back into the store and peeked out the window to see where she was. If she came into the store, I was a sitting duck. There was nowhere to hide.

Now she's reloading, and fires off another round up at the second floor. A piece of the house blew off. I hit the ground and belly-crawled to the front of the store to see if I could escape into the barbershop where there would be some adults.

As I peeked out the door, I heard police sirens blaring and prayed that they were coming for her. I decided to make a run for it, and like a character in a thriller spy movie, I hugged the building wall and schootched along to get to the barbershop, which was only about 10 feet away. Luckily, the sirens I heard were for her.

The police arrived, jumped out of their cars, and swarmed Wifey.

She was wrestled to the ground, handcuffed, arrested, and charged with a hot dog cart full of various and sundry crimes. A few months later, we threw in the towel and closed the store.

MY NEXT GIG

S o, our first business experience was a failure. Undaunted, my father went all in again, put up his house as collateral, and bought a well-established luncheonette in Rochelle Park, New Jersey. This place must have been in business for 50 years, and now the owner was retiring.

My mother worked lunch; I worked after school, and my 12-year-old brother worked on the weekends. I was now 17, had my own car, and did the work-study program at school. Rather than waste time in study hall, I crammed in all my required classes, got out of school early, and worked at the luncheonette as much as I could. During the summer, I worked 7 days a week. I loved working. I graduated high school in 1972, and my only interest besides girls was working and making money.

My parents had other ideas for me, and I was nagged into attending the local community college. Well, I registered and went to a few classes, but cut most of them. I soon approached my father and said, "Here's the deal, I'm not going to college anymore. Either hire me full time or someone else will." My dad understood. He had watched me hustle: cutting lawns, shoveling snow, working at three other retail stores, working at a vegetable stand, babysitting, buying and selling mini bikes then cars, delivering newspapers—you name it, I did it. I even bought paint and stencils and painted house numbers on curbs for 50¢. While my friends were hanging out, I was hustling. You see, my original goal was to become a millionaire by the time I was 18, but I had to keep pushing that age higher.

My father brought me on full time. I worked about 60 hours a week and opened the place every morning at 4:30 am. The counter was full by 5 am, and the business was in full swing.

I hustled everything in that store, from pots and pans that fell off trucks to any hot merchandise the truckers would sell me.

I'd sell you a watch or a cheeseburger, and it didn't matter to me as long as I was selling something.

My father paid me $150 per week, and within two years I saved $10,000. I thought I would invest the money I had saved into a real estate venture, so I put a deposit down on a small strip shopping center in Rochelle Park. For $85,000, I would own seven stores and a two-family house, which was included on the property. But there were problems—no credit, not enough money for a down payment, and no mortgage.

NEXT GIG

While still running the luncheonette, another opportunity presented itself that we had to act on—right now! A well-established diner in Westwood, New Jersey came up for sale. One of the owners committed suicide, and the place was looking for a buyer. We bought it for $42,500, put down $30,000 (Dad's $20K and my hard-earned $10K), and financed the rest. It was difficult to run two places effectively, so my father hired a manager for the luncheonette until he sold it about six months later.

Now I'm about 21 years old and the proud one-third owner of a well-established diner that was re-opening after having been closed for several months. The challenge was to let the public know that the diner had reopened, and the food and service would be great.

We hired a great chef named Bernie, who could bake and cook. He made a matzo ball soup that was better than sex (depending on your particular sex life). Within six or eight weeks, we had the place humming and began to turn a profit. We opened 24 hours on the weekends and captured the movie crowd. Owning this place made us feel like restaurateurs rather than just luncheonette guys.

A year passed, the business was up and running strong, so it was time to sell. We got a good offer, one that doubled what we had paid in just 12 months. We held a mortgage for the buyers and collected about $600 a month. My father received $400, and I got $200. This lasted for five years.

It took us about six months to find another business to purchase, so in the meantime I got a job at IBM in Franklin Lakes, New Jersey as a short-order cook. George, the chef, used to come in the diner and the luncheonette in Rochelle Park, so he was a friend of the family already.

He got me the job, although there must have been a waiting list for the position. IBM always had a great reputation, including benefits and all the bells and whistles that go with a great corporate job.

Within only a few months they promoted me to manager of their Mahwah branch. It was a much smaller operation, and I enjoyed working independently. My boss, Mr. Townsend, was a great guy and liked the way I worked. Later, he was our best customer in our next venture. I felt bad taking the position, knowing that any day we would be back in business, and I would leave.

Eight weeks later, they received my notice—we found our next business opportunity.

MY NEXT GIG

We received a call from a business broker telling us that a well-established luncheonette was for sale in Wyckoff, New Jersey and that the owner was retiring. The place had been in business for more than 60 years, it was a little run down, with lots of room for improvement. This is where we saw the opportunity. It was in a nice strip mall with lots of parking and in a great town.

In only a few months, we doubled the breakfast and lunch crowd and became incredibly successful. I did the short-order cooking, while my father worked the register, schmoozing everyone who came in. I took pride in firing out breakfast and lunch orders with lightning speed and still managed to make every dish look special. My brother Jack was still going to school, so he worked weekends to help us out.

I remember Jack rolled over his hot rod Barracuda on Route 208 on his way to work one weekend. The joke was that my father was pissed that he was late for work and that the crumb donuts he was going to bring to the luncheonette were crumbled from the accident. Jack wasn't hurt, so we were able to laugh about it later.

After two years, we flipped the business again, doubled what we paid for it and again held a mortgage for the next owner. Now, in addition to the diner mortgage we held, we also were collecting $1,000 a month ($500 each) for another five-year period. Not bad! Now I'm 25 and have $700 a month coming in without working and more than enough to cover the mortgage on a house that my wife and I bought just two years prior. That was nice change in 1979.

Now we set our sights on something bigger—maybe a large-capacity restaurant with a liquor license. And, maybe a place with a little music? My father, brother, and I wanted to do something together, and the timing seemed right. So our search began.

Again, between businesses I found a job as a short-order cook at a place in Ringwood, New Jersey called Morrissey's Country Kitchen. I only stayed for a few months, long enough to find our ultimate place.

CIRCUS-CIRCUS

Sometime in December 1978, my brother got word of a restaurant/bar named "Peanuts" in Bergenfield, New Jersey that was for sale. With 5,000 square feet of space, a banquet-sized kitchen, and a ton of parking, we quickly became interested. I remember our first visit to the place. We sat at a booth and were immediately welcomed with popcorn and peanuts, and a menu that seemed to cater to children. Cartoons were projected onto a wall as a kid's party was in full swing. (Does it sound like another place you know?) Let me give you a hint. Go ahead, throw your peanut shells on the floor. Yes, it was Ground Round Grill and Bar. Same idea, same concept, same peanuts!

The rest is all ROCK and ROLL!

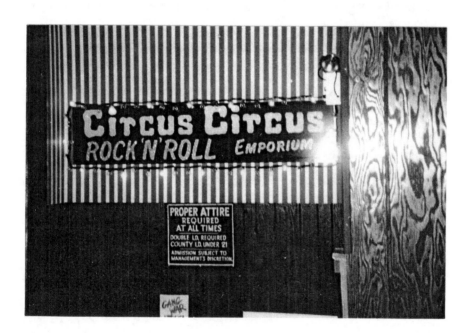

Forward Let's Rock

Ah, the brave foolishness of youth. Take an ambitious 25-year-old kid from a little suburban town in New Jersey, his music-obsessed kid brother, and a dad who believed in the whole idea. Add loud rock and roll, wet T-shirt nights, nickel beer, and here we are.

This book is a chronicle of those times, and a tribute to all the rock bands and club goers on the tri-state club circuit and around the country during the late 70s and 80s. From Ramsey to Carteret, from Hoboken and Fort Lee, to the little town of Bergenfield, it was a time of great clubs and even greater music.

While the scene in New York City was thriving, from Irving Plaza to Max's Kansas City and the Bottom Line, another scene was developing out in the suburbs, where young rock fans actually lived. Any night of the week, winter or summer, they were filling clubs to see their favorite bands—loud, hot, sweaty, and live.

Imagine a sitcom about this young kid who opens up a rock and roll nightclub at a time when the American music industry equaled GM or the NFL in terms of power and influence. That's what my world was like for five years—every day.

And it all happened in a converted restaurant-bar called Circus-Circus on Washington Avenue in Bergenfield, New Jersey.

There were nights when the kids lined up around the block, just to meet their friends and feel the volume of the bands right in their faces. They were there to blow their little paychecks, forget their McJobs, pound some beers, and maybe lock eyes and then lips with someone special on a crowded dance floor or pogo pit.

There were nights when it felt as if the music might rip your ears off and hand them to you. These musicians practiced in garages and warehouses and then come out to play for one reason and one reason only—"to kick your ass," as singer John Kay from Steppenwolf told me one warm June night before going on stage to rock yet another sold-out show at our club.

Heck, we were just luncheonette guys. That was our business before rock and roll—serving up burgers and fries to a working-class clientele. But we knew opportunity when we saw it.

Still, no one was more surprised than we were when we became one of the hottest clubs on the circuit and in the area.

Talk about glory days!

But fame is relative. Today's pop singer or alternative band has a predecessor in an earlier act—someone who first influenced and informed them. If you're pushing past 50, the names conjure fantastic images—cartoon-punk prototypes, The Ramones and metal crazies Twisted Sister, who danced the fine line between devils and dorks. If you're 20, please hand the book back to Gramps and step away from the Barcalounger.....please!

There was The Joe Perry Project, born from the ashes of the then-shattered Aerosmith. There was Hot Tuna's Jorma Kaukonen and country rock artists, New Riders of the Purple Sage.

There was the early shock rock of The Plasmatics, who made Marilyn Manson look like Justin Bieber.

So many more. Modern singer-songwriter Steve Forbert, soulful Rick Danko of The Band, former New York Doll Johnny Thunders, and his former mate, singer David Johansen, who later metamorphosed into Buster Poindexter.

You get the idea.

We had awesome cover bands too, including some who penned their own music. The names won't mean much now, but on a good night, they sent a lot of kids home happy.

White Tiger, Southern Cross, Friends, Badlands, Prophet, Courtney, Impact, Nines, Flossie, Trigger, Condor, Protégé, Molly Cribb, Nasty-Lass, Pegasus, Thorin Oak, Salty Dog, Clover Hill, Desperate Men, Saturday Night Special, Sundog, Blue Emerld, and so many others. If you were there, you remember them.

And there were the great tribute bands like Crystal Ship (The Doors), Rat Race Choir (Led Zeppelin), Dr. Jimmy and the Who Show, TT Quick (ACDC), Yasgur's Farm (Woodstock), Sticky Fingers (The Rolling Stones), Timberwolf (Grateful Dead), Backstreets (Bruce Springsteen), Nursery Cryme (Genesis), and Beatle Magic, who paid tribute to a little band from Liverpool.

If you closed your eyes, you'd think they were all the original artists. Crystal Ship even sold out the Capital Theater in Passaic, New Jersey. I don't think The Doors ever did that.

As it is with fame, memories are relative too. We all have them. Your kids will have them. But here's the difference: These memories are *yours*. Let's rock.

Blow Is Everywhere

News Item: The Bergen County Task Force last night arrested 25 suspects on drug charges just one day after Hudson County authorities announced the biggest cocaine seizure in their county's history.

Acting Bergen County Prosecutor Richard Carley said this morning that the Bergen suspects, arrested at scattered points across the county, were part of a drug distribution ring in which cocaine was a major part of the operation.

—Bergen Record, *December 16, 1982*

It's 1979. Cocaine, that insidious and powerfully addicting nasal decongestant, is flowing in and around the club scene just as fast and plentiful as water from a faucet. It was difficult to find anyone who worked in or near the club scene who wasn't using the drug regularly. The 2001 film, *Blow* starring Johnny Depp, lays the facts out pretty well. It's based on the true story of Carlos Lehder and his Medellin cartel, which specialized in smuggling cocaine from Columbia to the US on a huge scale. It was primarily responsible for most of the white powder coming into the US.

But they had help…everywhere. Even in my club. See, every joke, every cliché about the era is unfortunately true. If you were there, you know what I'm talking about. In the 1970s cocaine emerged on the scene as the new and fashionable drug that provided energy, prestige, and an invincible feeling. It was the drug of choice for entertainers, their fans, business people, Wall Street honchos, and their wealthy neighbors. College campuses all over America saw an explosion of usage between 1970 and 1980 and the drug traffickers knew it. They set up elaborate networks to get the coke into the U.S. by the ton to satisfy the soaring demand.

From the men's and ladies rooms, to the bands' dressing area, to the parking lot, to just about anywhere, it was here. I couldn't sniffle without someone coming up to me, pointing their finger to one nostril simulating snorting coke in a positive, kind of congratulatory way, as to say, "You do blow?"

It wasn't unusual for band members, roadies, and customers to ask me if I wanted to do a line.

Fast forward. It's Wednesday, December 15, 1982, Christmas season. It's cold, about 21 degrees, with winds blowing in from the north at about 10 mph. The club is maybe a third full. There were two cover bands on stage, Dreamer and Tursha.

One of my employees yells in my ear that I have a phone call. I make my way back to the office, away from the music, and grab the phone. It's a friendly voice.

"Hi, is Joe around? This is Bob."

"Oh, yeah, sorry, this is Rick. You want me to get him?" "Nah, that's OK. I'll just come by in a little bit. Tell him to sit tight. Thanks!"

I grabbed a seat at the bar next to Joe.

"Your friend Bob called. Said he'd be by in a minute." Joe's face cracked. He had this look of being queasy and scared and brave all the same time. I suddenly felt like he looked.

"Yeah, okay, cool," he said.

About 20 minutes later, five agents from the Bergen County Narcotics Task Force burst through the front and rear entrances, started barking orders, and then began handcuffing and arresting people.

Among those arrested were five employees of The Circus, including Joe. He was arrested and charged with distributing a controlled, dangerous substance, and conspiracy. This means you have a lot of cocaine, you're selling it regularly, and your buddies are helping you.

One-by-one they were handcuffed, put into unmarked cars, driven to the county jail, and placed in jail cells. *The Bergen Record* reported the next morning that the raid also took in the main local dealer, a guy with a connection that stretched all the way back to Colombia.

Though this all took place under my nose, I really had no knowledge of the scale of what was happening. So many years after the fact, I would tell you if I did.

I later learned that my home phone was tapped and several conversations had been intercepted. A small team of agents had been actually watching Joe's high-rise apartment in Hackensack with high-powered binoculars for months. Though they had nothing on me, it was still unnerving to think that I was being watched that entire fall. Following the arrests, it was beginning to look like the end. A couple of years are a huge difference in the life of a 20-year-old, and as my regulars moved on to marriage and new lives, fewer kids replaced them. The long lines of customers that used to wrap around the building were gone, the drinking age was about to increase to 21, and the nation was wilting under a stubborn recession, the worst since the Great Depression. With unemployment at record highs, the kids didn't have the money to go out partying five or six nights a week like they used to. Interest rates and inflation were skyrocketing. (Federal Reserve interest rates at year end were 11.5% and inflation rose to 16%.) Nothing was going our way any longer.

My employees and friends were actually in jail. The walls seemed to be closing in on me. I used one credit card to pay another. Where did it all go? We'd been on top of the world, and now that world was pushing us down. We were desperate. As the cash flow dwindled, we needed money to keep afloat. But the banks weren't lending money, especially if you wanted it for a business. One day, I saw a newspaper ad offering private business loans—just a guy offering loans. In desperation, we paid 24% interest for a 1-year, $25,000 loan. This "private lender" even asked us to pay "points" as well (one percent of the loan amount to give the lender an even higher yield). With my father in this guy's office in Fair Lawn, New Jersey, we didn't even ask questions, and he didn't ask us any questions. There was just one agreement to sign—the one that said he would own our houses if we defaulted. We postdated four checks, one for each quarter of the year, and somehow paid the loan back on time. I'm sure this guy was hoping we wouldn't be able to pay.

Now the handwriting was on the wall. The drinking age would soon be 21. We took for granted that the thousands and thousands of kids we could potentially draw from area colleges would always be there. But soon, 75- to 80% of them would no longer be old enough to drink.

Ironically, early on, there was actually a time when I hoped our business would slow down. Though we were riding a huge wave of success and popularity, I sometimes had this paranoia that we were drawing too much attention. Night after night, we were pushing the envelope and packing the place to over capacity. This created fears in the back of my mind that something bad would happen. Would it be a fire or an over-zealous bouncer hurting someone really badly? It had to end. We knew it would. Maybe not on our terms, but we got out with our pants still on. Barely.

But oh, how we rocked.

On With the Show, This is It

"I wish that I knew what I know now, when I was younger...."
—Ronnie Lane, The Small Faces

There was a local bar on Washington Avenue in Bergenfield called "Peanuts"—it had a jukebox, a bar, two pinball machines, and two cigarette machines. We were opening up a rock and roll club. Would we really need much else? But we didn't. It was 1979. I was 25, my brother 20, and my father, 54. We saw opportunity.

It wasn't really like we were kids. I had worked at something, anything, since I was in grade school. Our family had experience with the little diner here, the little luncheonette there. We worked hard. I could flip a pretty mean hamburger, and I was good with money. My brother knew every band. To our young minds, it all made sense.

We paid $175,000. This got us the bar and the liquor license. We closed the bar for two weeks to do some low-budget renovations; we built three bars, created a big shiny dance floor, put up some lights, and built a halfway decent stage with an industrial-strength sound system. If we were gonna play rock and roll, we were gonna play some rock and roll. And we were gonna play it THIS LOUD.

There we were, four days before opening the place, and we were basically broke. We barely had enough cash on hand to stock the bar. To sell beer, we had to buy a lot of it. We emptied the pockets of our jeans and dresser drawers just to have enough petty cash on the four registers. It's Sunday, March 11. We're t-minus four days before the doors would open for the first time as Circus-Circus, and our private by-invitation-only party was about to begin. Cooks prepared hot and cold food that you could smell just coming up the stairs. The waitresses and bartenders were dressed, every hair in place, and eager to pour for our 125 invited well-wishers. It was graduation, the first day of school, Christmas, and final exams all at the same time.

We were changing a restaurant-bar into a serious, major league rock club, and just the thought made me as nervous as a cat in a room full of rocking chairs. And, I won't mention how many sleepless nights I worked the numbers and tried to figure out what it would take to pay the bills and turn a profit.

Opening to the public was only four days away and this was our Super Bowl. Everything we'd worked for and earned in three prior businesses was all riding on a club called Circus-Circus.

The grand opening party was great, not just because of the good time everyone seemed to have, but because it gave us an opportunity to have a dry run and work out some kinks. Everything seemed to work. The food was great, the music rocked, and people seemed to really like the place, all 125 of 'em.

We advertised our public grand opening on one of the biggest rock stations in the largest radio market in America—WPLJ in New York. This was huge. At the time, WPLJ in NYC, WMMS in Cleveland, WBCN in Boston, and KMET in Los Angeles represented the state of American rock radio. A steady diet of Pink Floyd, Lynrd Skynrd, Foreigner, Styx, Kansas, and a host of other popular bands kept their loyal audiences growing. These were our people.

In addition, we ran print advertising in *The Aquarian Weekly*, New Jersey's rock bible, the local "who's who" for Jersey clubs and bands. Since 1969, if it rocked in New Jersey, it was in *The Aquarian*.

The advertising wasn't cheap, but I still could never have imagined that 435 people would show up on that first cold night. It was 32 degrees in Bergenfield that Thursday, but the lines easily stretched from the door out into that cold windy evening. I thought if we could get 100 people the first night that would be good. It was bedlam. We had only three bouncers and three bartenders on duty. We ran out of beer in the first two hours and had to borrow some from a local liquor store where my brother knew the owner—quite illegal according to the Alcoholic Beverage Control, as we learned later.

You are cordially invited to attend

the pre-Grand Opening Party

at the new

"Circus-Circus"

(Restaurant-Night Club)

Sunday, March 11th, 1979

Hours: 1:00 - 5:00 P.M.

52 So. Washington Avenue
Bergenfield, N.J. 07621

Jack Bandazian
Ricky Bandazian
Jack Jr. Bandazian

Badlands, a local cover band, played country rock music that seemed to ignite the crowd. It was that kind of an audience: shit-kickers in muscle cars, flared hair, and down vests—the kind of people Bruce Springsteen wrote about, with none of the literary romantic notions.

Oh, but it was glorious. There were at least three fights before the night ended, one of which tumbled out into the streets with my brother and I doubling as bouncers. Not that I could stop anyone. Checking in at 5 foot 6 inches tall, 150 pounds soaking wet with platform shoes, I was no one to be fighting 6-foot-tall dudes with "beer muscles" and who knows what else in them. My brother, on the other hand, was 20 years old, 6 feet tall, and 220 pounds of solid muscle. A high school wrestling star and street fighter, he feared nothing and no one. Even my 6'7" bouncers didn't want to mess with him. (Whenever I wanted to fire a bouncer, I let my brother do it. Either that or I would send them a neatly-typed memo.) Anyway, we got through that first night and had a cash register packed full of money. We literally had to empty it out several times that night. There was no such thing as a credit card in those days. That was a good thing!

Based on what we learned opening night, we quickly made some adjustments and prepared for a capacity crowd on Friday and Saturday. In 48 hours, we bought enough cases of beer and booze to construct a small house. We hired bouncers, we hired waitresses, and we hired bartenders. That weekend, about 1,600 paid customers climbed up the stairs from the rear parking lot and through our doors. The line was out the door the entire weekend. When two customers left, we would let two more in, except of course, when my brother was at the door. Then, it was more like two out and three in. That customer line extended around the building for two straight years. Every night seemed to be The Greatest Night on Earth.

How hot were we? When the Three Mile Island nuclear accident happened in nearby Dauphin County, Pennsylvania, we landed tens of thousands of dollars in catering orders from the cleanup crew. When you're hot, you're hot.

"Grand Opening"

OF

Circus-Circus

THUR. MARCH 15
'BADLANDS'

SPECIAL ADM. $1

FRI. MARCH 16
'IMPACT'

SAT. MARCH 17
NASTY-LASS

EVERY WED.- SUPER GREASER

COMING SOON

PEGASUS
CONDOR
COURTNEY

FRIENDS
WOODROSE
IMPACT
DESPERATE MEN

THORIN OAK
FLOSSIE
SUN DOG

Before computers

Daredevils and Snake Charmers

We kind of thought of ourselves as trailblazers. Everyone says this, and every bar would like to think this, but we had all the crazy stuff going on before most clubs. Clearly, our experience showed how crazy *we* were. But in a money contest, my cash is often on the guy with googly eyes in a suit made of buffalo wings, and springs on his shoes. That's the guy who will do anything.

We always wanted to be the first at everything. Sometimes it paid off, and sometimes it sank out of sight. But as my father always said, "If you want to launch big ships, you have to go where the water's deep!" We spent years searching for deeper waters.

Usually bands tried to pass me a demo tape, because they wanted to play at the club or maybe just open for one of the big acts. Even though we usually booked through agencies, I felt everyone deserved a few minutes of my time, even though my brother had the final say regarding who would play at our club. He had a great track record of delivering huge talent, and I wasn't going to second-guess him.

So, this guy comes into the club one afternoon. That's how this story begins…

Here's this kid, I think his name was Dale, about 15 or 16 years old, sitting in a booth with me in the middle of a quiet afternoon.

"Dale," I said, "I don't want to be rude, but you have five minutes, and they start right now."

The kid looks me right in the face and says, "I'm the youngest daredevil escape artist in the world. I'll bring in a huge truck with a crane and hang upside down from a burning rope wearing a double straight jacket, 200 feet in the air. If I don't get out of both straight jackets within minutes, I'll fall to my death.

I'll have all the big TV stations here. They're always looking for something spectacular."

I was charmed, to be sure, but I replied, "That's cool, Dale, but I have two questions. 'How much?' and, 'Who the hell would insure you, because without insurance, I'm not interested.'"

The insurance carrier was Lloyd's of London. Lloyds of London, in case you don't know, is world-renowned for insuring just about anything. Like these things, according to the website, howstuffworks.com

- In 1957, world-famous food critic Egon Ronay wrote and published the first edition of the *Egon Ronay Guide to British Eateries*. Because his endorsement could make or break a restaurant, Ronay insured his taste buds for $400,000.
- While playing on Australia's national cricket team from 1985 to 1994, Merv Hughes took out an estimated $370,000 policy on his trademark walrus mustache, which, combined with his 6 foot 4 inch physique and outstanding playing ability, made him one of the most recognized cricketers in the world.
- From 1967 to 1992, British comedian and singer Ken Dodd was in the *Guinness Book of Records* for the world's longest joke-telling session. He told 1,500 jokes in three and a half hours. Since then, he's sold more than 100 million comedy records and is famous for his frizzy hair, ever-present feather duster, and extremely large buck teeth. His teeth are so important to his act that Dodd had them insured by Lloyd's for $7.4 million, surely making his insurance agent smile.

So, a guy hanging from a crane? Please. No problem. The cost was $350. We shook hands, and the gig was set. We promoted it on radio, print, and inside the club. We promoted it like the Second Coming. Better than the Second Coming, since we had a contract.

Now it's Saturday, it's daylight, for God's sake, and the show was to start at 1 pm. By noon there must have been 500 to 600 people in our back parking lot waiting for this crazy stunt kid to show up. An ambulance was in the lot adding to the drama, along with a police contingency and several news crews, cameras ready. Right on cue, a white limousine turns the corner onto Washington Avenue and heads toward our parking lot. By now, it's about 2:30 pm, an hour and a half *after* the stunt was supposed to start. Even better, there are now close to 1,500 people in the parking lot. Dale slowly gets out of the limo, coolly walks up to a makeshift stage, and begins to address the crowd for half an hour.

It was the usual carney midway stuff. "Ladies and gentlemen, should I crash to the pavement, and splatter my soul and all my intestines on this pristine parking lot, and I don't see you again, thanks for coming out. Please know that you are my favorite audience ever!" It was that sort of thing. It was like Evil Knievel performing one of his stunts—1 hour and 58 minutes of talk and commercials, and two minutes of stunt. Finally, Dale puts on the double straight jacket and is hoisted up the crane from the rope, upside down. When he gets to 200 feet, they somehow light the rope, and his assistants act like something is suddenly going terribly wrong. Part of me is thinking, "Oh, here comes the shtick…" and the other half is saying, "Hmmm…really?" It did make me think.

He escaped (in the nick of time!), the show was a huge success, and we got unbelievable PR exposure. At least two major local networks covered and broadcast the story. I was getting tons of calls from people telling me they saw it on the news. For at least a day, the stations would end each news broadcast with the story. And, of course, the lower third on the screen read, "From the parking lot of Circus-Circus, Bergenfield, New Jersey." For $350 and some advertising costs, we got a million dollars in publicity!

Actually, we tried our hand at just about anything we thought would fly…including female mud wrestling, of course. The date was February 7, 1981…maybe you were there!

They were called the "Chicago Knockers," and you would know why if you saw this group of beautiful women in their skimpy bathing suits with names such as, Raging Apache, Killer Kelly, and Bone Crusher Bonnie. The action took place on the stage in a pool filled with mud. A pair of wrestlers were matched up against one other as an emcee egged them on, along with a houseful of drooling young guys just hoping and praying that a bathing suit top would be pulled off during the match.

The show usually consisted of three or four wrestling matches with the crowd determining the winner by applause. At some point in the show, a male volunteer from the audience would be coaxed into giving it a shot in the pit with a wrestler, and on occasion, we even had a guest celebrity.

That's when it got crazy. How crazy? Crazy enough that The New Jersey Athletic Control Board ordered The Chicago Knockers to cancel two South Jersey engagements, because the ladies didn't have professional wrestling licenses, according to *Enquirer* staff writer, Laura Quinn. The promoter for the Knockers stated in the article that the wrestlers had performed in all 50 states, including Six Flags Great Adventure Amusement Park and had never been prevented from staging a show by a state athletic commission.

"It's not billed as professional wrestling. We didn't think it fell under the state's jurisdiction," he stated. If they were to be categorized as "wrestlers" then certain rules were to apply, such as a state wrestling inspector would have to be on hand during performances along with a host of other requirements. Well, at least our show came off without a hitch. I seem to recall we did okay that night financially.

Then we tried to get something going on Sunday night—male burlesque. Of course, right? They were called "Morris's Mixed Nuts" You get the point. Talk about successful. About 150 to 250 screaming ladies would show up on a night that we were usually closed. It was $5 to get in, and we raised the prices of our drinks by 25¢. That was quite a high cover charge more than 30 years ago.

Besides a couple of waitresses serving cocktails to the screaming ladies, we had Danny Dooner, a tall, good-looking muscular, 18 -year-old kid from Glen Rock, who would sometimes double as a beer runner, bouncer, waiter, or whatever we needed. When we had the male review on Sunday nights, he would wait on tables and had the ladies going crazy. His entire uniform was just a bow tie, no shirt, and black pants. There is a line in the first *Godfather* movie where Moe Green, a Vegas casino owner, is being bought out by the Corleones. Asked to explain why he was "slapping Freddy" (brother of Michael Corleone) around, he replied, "He was banging cocktail waitresses two at a time. Players couldn't get a drink at the table!" That was Danny. He had his pick of any woman in the place.

And then there was the infamous snake show. One evening a guy pulled his car into our rear parking lot, and a small crowd began to form. I made my way down the back stairs into the lot to see what the commotion was about, and I noticed that his trunk is open. Looking a little closer I saw a bunch of live snakes loose in his trunk hissing and slithering around.

"What are you doing?" I said to the owner of these slimy creatures. He told me he raised king cobras and was interested in doing a show at the club. His shtick, if you will, was to charm (essentially play with) four or five of these venomous and sometimes deadly snakes at the same time in front of an audience. He also told me that, should he be bitten, he would have about 30 to 45 minutes to get to a hospital and get an injection of antivenin, although, survival depended on the amount of venom injected into his system from the bite.

Here's how it goes down: the venom, a complex mixture of proteins and enzymes, enters your body either subcutaneously or intramuscularly. Neurotoxins may then travel through the lymphatic system and begin to work on your nervous system, causing muscle paralysis. Hemotoxins then begin to break down your blood and tissue. Nephrotoxins may travel to your kidneys and cause acute tubular necrosis, destroying the tubes that carry waste from your blood to your bladder. Cardiotoxins, or blood poisons, may affect your heart muscles. Muscle fibers from dying flesh may enter your bloodstream and affect your kidneys, creating a condition called Rhabdomyolysis. Meanwhile, the area around the bite fills with excess fluid in a condition called edema. Ecchymoses, a bruising or discoloration from damaged capillaries, starts to occur. As blood cells are destroyed, a condition called thrombocytopenia—the ability of the body to transfer oxygen to the kidneys—is reduced, also causing acute tubular necrosis ("necro" generally means something is dying) in the kidneys. Blood pressure drops to dangerous levels. In some cases, a severe allergic reaction may occur. Anaphylaxis occurs when the body's immune system begins to compensate by overproducing antibodies in response to the presence of a foreign protein. In cases of anaphylactic reactions, the person may exhibit hives, cyanosis (a bluish discoloration to the face), and swelling of the throat that causes an inability to breathe. The possibility of death occurs within minutes.

Suffice it to say that snakebites are pretty nasty business.

But none of this happened.

The show was actually kind of a flop. Not very charming and certainly (and fortunately) no snakebites.

Interestingly enough, I read in the newspaper years later that this same guy was rushed to a hospital and almost died from a king cobra bite. This, according to the news article, was the second or third time he'd been bitten. This, my friends, is also why you never see a newspaper headline saying, "World Faces Massive Stupidity Shortage."

Pinball, Video, and Cigarette Machines!
Ka-ching!

When you put the quarter in the slot and hear that familiar sound of bells ringing, lights flashing, and that thumping sound, you know you're about to test your skills at pinball. Sometimes it's just you and the machine and other times it's you, the machine, and spectators. There's a sense of added pressure to do well when people are watching, especially when the champion is right next to you and waiting for you to lose so he can take the machine. After all, there are only three pinball machines, one video game, and 10 people waiting to play. But it wasn't always like that.

If you wanted to play pinball in New York in the 1950s and 1960s, you were out of luck. That's because it was outlawed in most of America's big cities, according to an article written by Seth Porges in *Popular Mechanics* titled, "11 Things You Didn't Know About Pinball History." The article goes on to state the reason for the bans:

> *Pinball was a game of chance, not skill, so it was a form of gambling. Pinball really did involve a lot less skill in the early years of the game, mostly because the flipper wasn't invented until 1947... five years after most of the bans were implemented. Up until then, players would bump and tilt the machine in order to sway the ball's gravity. Many lawmakers believed pinball to be a mafia-run racket as well as a time-and-dime-waster for impressionable youth. In New York, the pinball ban was executed in a particularly dramatic fashion. Mayor Fiorello La Guardia issued an ultimatum to the city's police force stating that their top priority would be to round up pinball machines and arrest their owners. He proceeded to spearhead massive prohibition-style raids in which*

thousands of machines were rounded up in a matter of days before being smashed with sledgehammers by the Mayor and police commissioner. The machines were then dumped into city rivers.

Similar scenes are reminiscent from the television show *The Untouchables*, which ran in the late 1950s and early 1960s showing the same determination of law enforcement to tackle prohibition lawlessness.

EARLY MARCH, 1979

It was just minutes ago that we had closed on the purchase of the bar, and the ink was barely dry on the documents. We left the attorney's office excited and couldn't wait to get back to the place and execute our plans for its transformation. The ride from Paterson to Bergenfield felt like an eternity; we finally got there, pulled into the rear lot of the building, and strolled in as the new proud owners. It was an eerie feeling turning the lock for the first time and walking into such a dark, quiet, and spacious place. Coming from a 1,000 square foot luncheonette and into a 5,000 square foot space seemed overwhelming at the time. I took the long walk from the rear of the building to the front door that faces busy South Washington Avenue, unlocked the door, and waited for a series of appointments that we had made, including meetings with food vendors, liquor salesman, employee inter-views, and so on. The door couldn't have been open 10 minutes when a tanned and burley heavyset guy walked in and asked for the owner. After a friendly handshake and all the congratulatory bull shit bestowed on a new owner, he began talking. "We were the vending company servicing this bar before you bought this place, and we want to continue the service. This way you don't have any problems," he said.

"What do you mean problems?" I asked innocently.

He continued to explain, "When the cigarette machines jam or the pinball games break down, we're here the same day to fix them so you won't have any problems."

Was he sending up a test balloon to see my reaction to that question and adjust accordingly? It almost sounded like a subtle threat, but why jump to any conclusions? After all, the guy was really nice. But so was Don Corleone. Could all the rumors be true about the mob controlling the vending business? Do you know what they say about rumors? They're usually true! As quickly as those words had come from his mouth, he opened his checkbook with his left hand and held a pen in his right. "How can I help you guys? $5,000? $10,000?" he asked.

The entire 15 minute conversation took place in a rustic and dimly lit booth, illuminated by a red, oval tiffany lamp hanging in the middle of the table and only a few feet from The Joker Poker, and Charlie's Angels pinball machines. My father sat to my left and "Frank," the vendor, sat across from us.

When the subject came up about money, I kicked my father under the table. When you're undercapitalized to begin with, 5 or 10 grand sounded like a lot of money, especially in 1979. We had heard that it was common practice to be advanced money from the machines; but once you take it, you couldn't even think of changing vendors, no matter what the service was like.

I asked to be excused from the table so my father and I could talk in private. After all, it was a big decision taking 5 or 10 Gs from someone you met only five minutes ago. I was streetwise long ago and knew there were no free lunches.

We talked it over and wound up taking $5,000, signing something that resembled a note. I didn't think it was in our best interest to take any more until we saw how fast it would come back in quarters. As Frank stated, once the loan was paid back, we could get more. It was probably a write-off for the vendor and a good deal for us. I'll bet these guys lose money every year according to their tax returns.

I remember sitting with the "pick up guy" every Friday afternoon as the quarters were emptied into a huge funnel-shaped machine that counted them. The loud clanking of the coins bouncing on the chrome spinning plate was music to my ears.

My favorites were Asteroids and Missile Command. Both were released by Atari (one in 1979, the other 1980). Remember those? Addictive, right?

Beer bottles, cigarettes, and half-spilled drinks littered the smudged and stained glass of every pin ball, cigarette machine, and video game, which seemed to be broken all the time and for different reasons. Sometimes it was because some numbskull put a slug in the coin slot or a spilled drink or beer wound up in the electronics board.

The cash registers, the hot dog cart, and every vending machine in the place were dancing to the tune of thousands of dollars all night, every night.

'DIVO' LIVE!
But not at Circus-Circus

It was 1980, a short time before Devo released their third album *Freedom of Choice*, which included their smash hit "Whip It," when my brother shared some exciting news. "I just booked Devo. You know—the group that wears the flower pots on their heads?"

By this time, we already had an impressive resume of national talent under our belts, and with Devo added, it would only enhance our reputation as a cozy, small- to mid-sized venue with big acts. This rising punk/ new-wave band had already performed to a national audience on *Saturday Night Live*, so scoring them at Circus-Circus was good news.

As customary, the management of Devo sent their tour manager to check out the venue, inspect the facility, and go through a checklist of items such as ample power, stage access, and basic logistics for a show. My brother met with the band's manager on a Wednesday afternoon. Within five minutes, he received some bad news.

While there's nothing noteworthy about getting high, when it mattered most, we weren't high enough. The ceiling, that is, over the stage. We failed the inspection. The ceiling height over the stage wasn't high enough to accommodate their "energy domes," which many incorrectly called, "power domes or flower pots." It was commonly stated, "Devo is the group that wears the flower pots on their heads." Not so!

Anyway, the clear message that day was this: "The ceiling height above the stage ain't high enough. As persistent as my brother was, there was no way he could add height to the ceiling without cutting through the roof. But don't think it didn't enter his mind!

"John Kay and Steppenwolf" or Steppenwolf?

I pulled into the parking lot at the same exact time as my brother on a cool, rainy day in April 1980. Jack rushed to my open door and said, "I can book John Kay and Steppenwolf for June 25th." He had apparently just gotten off the phone with their booking agency and was still excited over the news.

I'm thinking, "You mean the group from LA that was on *The Ed Sullivan Show?* The group that sings "Born to be Wild," the classic garage rock song from the film *Easy Rider?* "Magic Carpet Ride?" "The Pusher?" Holy shit!

Within a week, the posters went up on the walls, we had advertising on the radio and in the local papers, and we had unbelievable bragging rights. The rock group Friends, which was billed as New Jersey's #1 party band, was tapped to be the opener.

Several years after their first hits, Steppenwolf could apparently still bring the fans running. The show quickly sold out in advance, with people already scalping tickets two weeks before the show. I got all the money in advance from ticket sales, and we were sitting pretty. There was just one problem. The tickets said "Steppenwolf featuring John Kay." But, it wasn't "Steppenwolf featuring John Kay" that was planning to show up for the gig. It was some bogus band calling themselves Steppenwolf, with three of the original members—Nick St. Nicholas, Godly McJohn, Kent Henry, and a new lead singer, Tom Pagan.

No offense, guys, but you ain't Steppenwolf.

Any three knuckleheads, even "original" knuckleheads, could get a new singer and call themselves Steppenwolf. (In fact, in 1978, there was yet another band that called themselves Steppenwolf with a different lead singer and other original members of the group.)

But Steppenwolf *was* John Kay (nee Joachim Fritz Krauledat). End of story. No one was chomping at the bit to see his former bass player.

Now the drama began, and we were in the middle of it. As I said to my brother at the time, "The good news is that the show is sold out. The bad news is that the show is sold out." Customers were offering ticket holders three to four times face value to see John Kay and Steppenwolf, not three dudes that just called themselves Steppenwolf. Not only did I believe the fans would burn down our place when they looked up at the stage and saw "Live on Stage! Four Knuckleheads calling themselves Steppenwolf, but without Mr. Kay!" We were going to look like idiots.

We felt duped, but we knew we had to deliver. I still don't know today if this promoter was knowingly ripping us off with a bogus Steppenwolf. Or maybe to him, they weren't bogus.

Somehow, and now I can't remember all the details, but a tiny miracle took place. Through our contacts, we reached either the management of the real John Kay and Steppenwolf, or their promoter.

When John Kay himself found out about our dilemma, he went ballistic. This wasn't the first time this had happened.

The story, I'm told, was that John Kay had an agreement with his band members back in the early 70s, that if anyone left the band, that member forfeited any rights to the band name. When the group disbanded in 1972, (they reunited briefly in 1974), John Kay and drummer Jerry Edmonton were the last two standing. They thereby inherited the exclusive rights to the use the name. (Edmonton died in a car accident in Santa Ynez, California in 1993. He was 47.)

But, from 1977 to 1980, another concert promoter, we'll call him "Mr. Scumbag," put a variety of bands called Steppenwolf on the road as well. Unfortunately, we had our own history with this guy. He once took a deposit of $775 from us, promised us the English hard rock group Humble Pie, but never delivered on it. We only found out we were stiffed the night of the show when no one showed up, and Mr. Scumbag, of course, was nowhere to be found. (I still have a signed copy of the promissory note dated 5/10/1982, with his signature, just in case anyone wants to challenge me on the facts.) We never got our deposit back. What a shock. This type of thing was far more common than I knew. I had heard stories of promoters buying the "rights" to various band names, hiring musicians to fill out the bands, and then taking the whole imitation package on the road. It's legendary that back in the 70s, there were several groups called The Coasters crisscrossing the nation playing shows.

But now, back to our story, currently in progress.

John Kay and Steppenwolf, possibly out of spite and partly out of the desire to deliver to their fans, agreed to do the show for us, provided we flew the band and their significant others in from Boston, put them up in hotels, provided meals, a car service—the whole ride. It was a bargain.

Even though it was a sold out show, we probably broke even that night, and it was so worth it.

I'll never forget when they hit the stage. They came out with guns blazing.

JOHN KAY & STEPPENWOLF

Autographed to my sister Lori

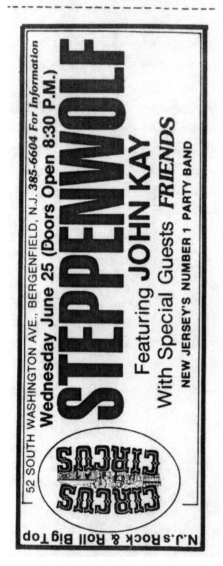

"Magic Carpet Ride" came first, then "Born to be Wild." The chills were going up and down my spine. It was crystal clear and sounded like I was listening to a record.

Then came "The Pusher."

The crowd was so into them, the floor began to move. I was actually scared the floor was going to give way and everyone was going to wind up in the basement. I jumped on top of a beer cooler in fright because the floor was moving up and down so noticeably. With "Born to be Wild," everyone in the place was jumping at the same time. It was so scary and apparent to me that something had to be done that after that show, we immediately hired an engineer to put up lally columns—round, structural steel columns filled with concrete—for better support. Fans could jump up and down all they wanted now.

It was one of those memorable shows I'll never forget. If only the fans knew what we went through to deliver.

As for John Kay, he was a really cool guy and easy to talk to. Before the concert, he said to me, "We're going to kick their asses!" And they did. All of our asses.

Only the Strong Survive

So, there we were. It was another Friday night, about 11 p.m., and the dance floor was packed. The music was hot and loud, and of course, the liquor was flowing. The band's rocking the place. The cash registers seem to ring in time to the music. It's a beautiful fall night in October 1979. What could go wrong?

Glancing up from my post at the bar, I suddenly saw—to my horror—Bergenfield police officers rushing the front and back doors, shotguns drawn.

Rewind to October 19, 1978. Jerry Randolph, age 28, a local ne'er-do-well and motorcycle club dude from nearby Englewood, got into it with another customer and was tossed out by bouncer Christos Eftychiou, age 24. This was in the club's earlier incarnation—a place called Peanuts Tavern—about a year before we bought the bar, but the memories were still fresh. Trouble doesn't care whose name is on the deed.

Randolph went home that autumn evening, rounded up three friends and came back to the club. Before the night was over, bouncer Eftychiou was dead, just three days after his 24 birthday, shot by Randolph. Another customer, Leonard Furst, was on his way to the hospital with a gunshot wound to the stomach.

(Not that it has anything to do with this particular evening, but Randolph, who'd been sentenced to life in prison for his role in the events of that October evening, managed to walk away from a work detail at Leesburg State Prison some years later.)

My heart was pounding as I managed to stop one of the officers to ask what the hell was going on. He said someone had called the police and reported that a patron in our club had a gun. It wasn't true, but this is what I think happened: one of my friendly competitors had made the call just to create panic and chase out customers. That was the scene back in those days. Several successful clubs in the area were competing for every

iller of bouncer escapes
from low-security prison

A 28-year-old convicted murderer
of a bouncer from a Bergenfield bar
escaped from Leesburg State Prison
yesterday morning while on a work
detail.

Jerry Randolph, who was serving
a life sentence for the fatal shooting
of Christos Eftychiou, 24, of Bergenfield in a bar fight in 1978, walked
away from other inmates and
guards at the minimum-security
prison about 10 a.m.

Authorities believed Randolph
was heading for the Trenton area to
join old friends who are members of
a motorcycle gang. Leesburg is located in Cumberland County in
South Jersey.

"We have an idea of where he is,
and we'll get him," a prison official
said last night.

Randolph, who lived in Englewood, shot Eftychiou in Peanuts
Tavern at 52 S. Washington Ave.
Oct. 19, 1978. Randolph had returned
to the bar with three friends after
being ejected by Eftychiou earlier in
the evening for fighting.

Randolph also shot a bar patron,
Leonard A. Furst Jr. of Lake Hopat-
cong, in the stomach. Furst recov-
ered.

— TOM TOOLEN

last customer; kicking, clawing, and throwing out all the rules,
until only a few clubs remained.

If it drew customers, clubs were doing it. First, one club
began "Ladies drink free until 10 pm." At another, it was "Ladies
drink free until midnight." Our gimmick? Nickel Beer Night. It
was just as crazy as it sounds. All the tap beer you could drink
from 8:30 to 9:30 pm for five cents. Imagine doing that today.

Actually, since then the idea of Ladies' Night has kept a lot
of lawyers in business. State courts in California, Maryland,
Pennsylvania, and Wisconsin have ruled that Ladies' Night discounts are unlawful gender discrimination under state or local
statutes. At the same time, courts in Illinois, Minnesota, and

Washington rejected a variety of challenges to these discounts, so the question remains open. Suffice it to say that Ladies' Night eventually became only a great deal for attorneys.

Here's how we did it for a few summers: every Thursday night featured Protégé, a terrific and popular band, with their hot lead singer, Sandi. Their presence alone guaranteed a great night. The first 200 people in the door got a free Circus-Circus T-shirt. Then, everyone in the place drank free. Yes *free* from 8:30 to 10:30 pm Then, the bikini contest would start about midnight. At 10:31, it was like turning on a cash machine for us.

You can imagine what the place was like by then. You're drinking for free for two hours, the band is packing the dance floor, and the bikini contest hasn't even started yet. Women are filling up the place to enter the contest, the dance floor is full, your friends are there, and the only happier place in the universe is Disneyland. And this was *every* Thursday night for several summers.

The bikini contest was an adventure ride all by itself. First prize was $100, second prize was $50, and third prize was $25. That was a lot of money back then, so there was never a shortage of girls willing to show almost anything. (For those of you keeping score, that $100 is equal to about $287 today, a pretty penny for a college kid.) Each contestant received a free sleeveless "I entered the Circus bikini contest" T-shirt. Nothing was better publicity than a pretty girl wearing our name on a T-shirt at the Jersey Shore that weekend.

Our bouncer, Ron, was a huge body builder. He acted as emcee, working the crowd like children at a puppet show. The rules were easy—the girl who generated the most noise won. He was a master at bringing the noise up every hot, crowded Thursday night.

Every week, on cue, as another stunning young woman walked away with the prize, Ron would ask the guys in the audience if any one of them could maybe give the winner a ride home, because she didn't have a car. Every male hand in the room shot up like a rocket.

We can only presume that somewhere—in one out of every dozen homes in Jersey from Fort Lee to Cresskill—there is a photo in the bottom drawer of a young, happy, bikini contest winner, now happily basking on her retirement porch, worried about her grandchildren and that crazy Internet.

But every great story has a villain. In our case, it was the Alcoholic Beverage Control ("The ABC"). It was their thankless duty to keep clubs such as ours under control in what seemed to be a perfectly out-of-control world.

The ABC told us we couldn't advertise "via any media, which utilizes promotional schemes unduly designed to increase the consumption of alcoholic beverages." In English, that meant, "You know those promotions you're doing to bring in more customers and sell more drinks? Yeah? Well, don't do 'em anymore."

The playing field only got steeper from there.

0203-33-001-003

State of New Jersey
DEPARTMENT OF LAW AND PUBLIC SAFETY
DIVISION OF ALCOHOLIC BEVERAGE CONTROL
NEWARK INTERNATIONAL PLAZA
U.S. ROUTE 1-9 (SOUTHBOUND), NEWARK, N. J. 07114
(201) 242-0768

JOHN J. DEGNAN
ATTORNEY GENERAL

JOSEPH H. LERNER
DIRECTOR

July 9, 1979

Dickran, Inc.
t/a Circus, Circus
52 South Washington Avenue
Bergenfield, Bergen Co., N.J.   07621

Gentlemen:

Our attention has been directed to your recent advertisement through the media of
, which included the following:

Recent newspaper ad - "Every Wednesday, 5¢ beer night, 8:30 - 9:30."

It has been the stated opinion of this Division and consequently its policy for many years
that any advertising, regardless of the media, which utilizes promotional schemes unduly designed to increase the consumption of alcoholic beverages is violative of N.J.A.C. 13:2-23.16.

The number and variety of types of advertising promotional plans unsuccessfully utilized by
licensees are too numerous to be listed hereon. However, they run the gamut from cocktail
hours; special nights, jumbo drinks to free food.

This Division will not tolerate these advertising schemes which are unduly designed to lure
patrons into licensed establishments. To allow such advertising would in our view, open a
dangerous door to larger or greater "give-aways" in order to attract patrons to licensed
premises. Opening of competition of this kind amongst retailers would be inconsistent with
any sound system of liquor control.

You are herewith placed on notice that this or similar types of advertisements must not be
repeated hereafter. In the event that any future violations are brought to our attention,
proceedings may be instituted and this warning together with any other violation will be considered in assessing penalties.

You must, therefore, let us have your prompt assurance by return mail that you have positively
discontinued such prohibitive advertising and will not engage in such or similar advertisements in the future.

Very truly yours,

JOSEPH H. LERNER, DIRECTOR

By: Anthony N. Frattini
    Assistant Deputy Director

My Tribe, Your Tribe: It's all About Sex

It's Wednesday night, a school night, a work night. But you're young, you're restless, full of energy, and it's only 10 pm. Where do you go tonight? Emerald City, Mother's, The Cuss from Hoe, The Soap Factory, The Final Exam, The Fountain Casino, or some other club?

It all depended on your tribe. And, wherever you went, you could expect to see hundreds of members of your tribe at any one of these venues.

I always marveled at how, as if by some unspoken code, every tribe dressed similarly, no matter how "outside" the norm or "outside the box" they were. It's like a baseball or hockey team. You can always tell which team they're on by their uniform.

If you're going to see a country rock band, you and your people wear a cowboy hat and boots, jeans (though not necessarily faded), and maybe a big buckle.

For a punk band, you'd have the skinny jeans, a ripped tee shirt, leather jacket, studded belt, a safety pin somewhere if you were true to the cause, spiked hair, spandex pants, and patches and buttons of other punk bands. Punks, ironically, wore a uniform like every other tribe. They were as tied to rebellion as the disco kids were tied to polyester. Punks seemed to attract other misfits with identity problems. They couldn't or wouldn't, be seen dressed in flannel or flares. That would be *so* uncool.

Still, no matter what tribe you were, whatever allegiance you claimed, you were out with your tribe for one reason—to hook up. Maybe my perspective is skewed, but it seemed that if you couldn't hook up back then, you were either lame, or you weren't there. Most didn't worry about contracting a disease, no less a deadly one.

During that time, no one had condoms on their shopping list. They seemed like something your Dad had, and you found them in his dresser drawer. (That changed quickly in the soon-to-follow era of AIDS, when condoms became a badge of honor.) When I went to school, if you were caught with a condom, you'd probably get suspended. Now, I think they give them out.

No matter the decade or generation, everyone likes to say that it was his or her era that brought on the sexual revolution. There has been a sexual vibe in every generation, from the '20's Paris to the Swinging '60s. To say you invented sexual freedom would be like claiming you invented taking lunch to work. Certainly the introduction of the Pill in the '60s removed a ton of fear from the idea of having sex, but the notion of "sexual freedom" might have just been really good word of mouth, a kind of social marketing.

Speaking of social marketing, our Internet consisted of you and you and him or her. There was face-to-face and lip-to-lip interaction all night long. Of course, today you can use that phone of yours—the one that contains nearly every fragment of gathered human knowledge since the dawn of time—and go to Match.com, e-harmony, ChristianSingle.com, Adultfriend-finder.com, and thousands of other dating and networking sites for people to meet, and yes, hook up!

By mid-2013, there were 40 million people dating online, with 17% resulting in marriages in the past year. The average customer spent $239 per year, adding to the more than one billion bucks spent annually on dating websites. According to statisticbrain.com (verified 6/18/2013) there are 54 million single people in the U.S., and almost 75% have tried online dating.

In fact, the numbers of Americans living alone has increased dramatically since the 1970s. And they're all sitting in front of their computers.

Need more proof? Or just a giggle? Here, thanks to the huffingtonpost.com, are some actual dating sites that almost cover the gamut of human interests and experiences. If you don't find your hook-up here, you might be missing some essential parts:

- **DiaperMates**. Yes, some people are into wearing diapers or are into dating other people who wear diapers. Waaah!
- **420Dating**. "Why toke alone?" their ad reads. A friend with weed and benefits is a friend indeed! "Don't bogart that joint, my friend. Pass it over to me/him/her…." (Gratuitous '70s marijuana tune reference.)
- **Pounced.com**. Do you have a desire to wear a furry suit? Are you a costumed unicorn nights and weekends? This site is a place for artists, writers, publishers, and fursuiters (people who like to dress in fur suits or anthropomorphic animal costumes for entertainment or pleasure).
- **Darwindating.com**. You better rock your species at this site or be prepared to be extinct. This site matches only those at the very top of the attractiveness food chain. You've been suitably warned.
- **UglyBugBall.com**. Does even your own mirror look away from you? Does your smile scare small children? Meet some of your own right here. Everyone else has been warned.
- **Farmersonly.com**. This site is huge in Nebraska. Wear your best overalls! This is for farmers and the farmers who love them. Looking for a roll in the hay? This might be the place. (Sorry. Seriously.)
- **WealthyMen.com**. Bring your checkbook. This site claims that its male members all make $100,000 a year and up. It makes no bones about it being a place for women who care more about the wallet in the back pocket than the package in the front. But hey, we don't judge.
- **MeetAnInmate.com**. Got a fetish for bars? The kind you live behind? This site pairs up women (most likely) with "attractive" incarcerated members of society for a meaningful and fulfilling relationship. If you don't mind not touching each other, like, ever, this site is for you.

So, here's where I'm going with this. Back in the day, you met at a bar, a club, or somewhere other than on a computer and exchanged home phone numbers that you either wrote down or memorized. Later maybe you hooked up or even married. It all happened in real time and in real life.

That's where you met people, plain and simple. It happened every single night at The Circus. Guys and gals felt safe with the Pill and worried very little about anything else. One customer even bragged to me how he had sex with four different girls in the same day. I don't know where you get that kind of energy! (On the other hand, he could have been lying.)

Frankly, if you were at Circus-Circus some night with your tribe, you were young, aware, cool, and about as attractive as you were ever going to be in your life. And, if you had weed, blow, or some other kind of drug, the magic words were simply, "Want to party?" This was code for "Ok, let's have some of this, and then find a place to have sex."

It seemed to work.

One of our bartenders, Steve, who was divorced and about 40 years old— enough to have kids the same ages as his cus-tomers—would always have a girl waiting for him at the end of his shift. Our policy was to allow each bartender and other help to have a guest stay at the end of the night for a drink after we closed and locked the doors. That was the real party, and every-one wanted to be there. It might be your girlfriend, boyfriend, husband, wife, or whomever. For some reason, Steve always had girls fighting over him. One "girlfriend" tossed a Coke in his face when she found out he was waiting for someone else for the after-party. We laughed about that for a long time.

Suffice it to say, the sex and drugs were everywhere; they permeated the place. Many late nights, the club simply reeked of marijuana, beer, perfume, and sex. It wasn't that we necessarily just allowed it all. As a licensed club, with some responsibilities, we actually tried to control it all. I had my bouncers go in and out of the men's room periodically to make sure no one was smoking. They should have been checking to see who *wasn't* smoking.

I was always paranoid because I was afraid the cops would come in and start arresting people. In addition to that concern, we had to worry about the ABC shutting us down or hitting us with a hefty fine.

The atmosphere always depended on the tribe. When you had a band like Timberwolf doing a Grateful Dead show, you would smell more weed than for, let's say, Friends, who was more of a party dance band. Some tribes just smoked more weed than others. The Deadheads were practically Rastafarian in their love of the Ganja.

The parking lot was another story—love shacks on wheels in the lot and for blocks around. Everywhere you walked, there were cars rocking with windows fogged up. My brother caught a couple going at it in the coat room, which was left unlocked during the summer months. Certainly no surprise there. The bands, of course, always had hot girls in the dressing room. But at least they could lock the door.

Remember that this was a time when the drinking age was 18, and we were situated between more than a few colleges, especially Fairleigh Dickinson in nearby Teaneck. (We even took out ads on their book covers.)

They provided us with a built-in crowd. These were kids away from home for the first time and now free to party whenever they wanted, as long as they had a few bucks or friends with a few bucks. (Or, even if they didn't!)

Their parents didn't know if they were studying or partying their asses off. Circus-Circus and other area clubs wouldn't have been attracting huge crowds on school nights if everyone was in their dorm studying.

No matter the night, no matter the crowd, no matter the band, no matter the tribe, they all found their way to Washington Avenue in Bergenfield.

I WAS THERE!

Whether you were at Circus-Circus or any other club during that special time, you know who you are. Maybe you were 18 years old and just out of high school or just finished your last class of the day at Fairleigh Dickinson, William Paterson, Montclair, Bergen Community, or any one of the dozens of colleges in the Tri-State area. Or you were just someone that wanted to see a great band and party. The toughest decision you had to make that evening was to decide which club to visit and which band you wanted to see. If you were with a group of friends, it usually required a vote. There were so many choices each night that some of the kids hit three or four different clubs in the same night and would end up seeing multiple bands. It was crazy…or so they tell me!

I heard one common theme over and over when I spoke to some of the club goers from back in the day, and it goes like this: "We lived through that era, and it's amazing that we survived!"

I reached out to some of the diehard rockers that were there in the late 70s and early 80s, and here's what they had to say about their time in the club scene. My questions to them are noted in bold text.

JAY O'BUCK
NEW YORK

I was 19 years old. Wherever there was a great show, I was there!

The Bottom Line, The Stone Pony, Mother's, The Red Rail, Fore-N-Aft, Lone Star Café; I went to all of them. I may have gone to Circus-Circus, but I can't remember, because we partied so much. All of those movies about the 70s parties; they're all pretty accurate. I remember going to Mother's, and still today can't remember if I got home that night. I think I woke up on someone's back porch somewhere. When it came to driving, I was always a passenger, so I could do whatever I wanted and have a great time.

I went to a lot of concerts at Madison Square Garden and have every ticket stub from every show mounted in a 4 by 5 glass frame. It's priceless...I couldn't even sell it. Ten Years After, Edger Winter, Eric Clapton; I've seen them all. I still go when I can catch a good act.

One night I saw Twister Sister, and they called it "anti-disco night." You'd bring your own record and everybody got to break it at the same time. Late 70s disco tried to rule, but it got squashed. They made the male gender feel like idiots wearing platform shoes and leisure suits. Later, everyone bought into that rap shit, which I wouldn't give you two cents for. That's what's out there, and kids are buying it. It's not their fault, because that's all they were really offered."

Would you say that you were part of the rowdy or mellow crowd?

I tried to stay away from the fights and trouble, but it seemed like it was all around us and in every bar. One night at a Port Chester club, this guy bit off someone's ear and got caught because he was showing it off at a local bar in Pleasantville, New York. He brought the ear in as a trophy.

Charming!

It was great times! I don't regret a single thing I did in those days. I can honestly say that.

VINNIE LANZA
NEW JERSEY

We went to all the Bergen County Clubs; whichever one was having the best band and the most women, that's where we'd go. It was a bunch of good times, a bunch of good sex, and a bunch of great rock and roll. That was it. That was my life inbetween college and sleeping sometimes only an hour before I went to work the next morning. We partied to the max. I could never do that today, but I did it back then. We looked forward to going out on the weekends and sometimes during the week. You had something to look forward to.

There was always a certain "man crowd" that seemed to get into the fights. It's like a protest. It's the same crowd that will show up and march, but they don't know why. You can

almost look at them and make the assumption. Were you one of the scrappers back then?

Oh yeah! I got into my share of fights.

And did the bouncers take care of you?

Oh, yeah!! There are still a few bars I go to in upstate New York that get a little crazy and remind me of the old times, especially because of the music the bands are playing. It's the same music we grew up with. It never gets old and is witnessed by its longevity. I rub elbows with people from 21 in age to 71 at these bars. We're all on the same page. When did that ever happen? Did you ever go to bar and see your parents there? I don't think so!

What's changed in the past few decades?

I can't even listen to the music that's out there today. It's just not the same.

What about the drug scene, past and present?

Back then we all smoked weed, some did coke and other things, but I still think there are more drugs out there today. Thank God we survived it all.

ROBERT (COCUNUT) DOUDOUKJIAN
NEW JERSEY

Do I think those days will ever come back? I wish! Just for one day! I really pray and wish on that!

If you liked great music, you went to Circus-Circus. I guess that's why I was there three or four nights a week. If I wasn't at that club, I'd be at L'Amour in Brooklyn, New York. That was another cool place. My girlfriend and I were just reminiscing about the club days. We didn't know each other back then, but I'm sure our paths crossed many times. We were both into the rock scene. I actually have pictures inside The Circus when Twisted Sister played there. I really miss the place.

What were your favorite bands?

Twisted Sister, The Joe Perry Project, The Ramones, Badlands, Flossie, and some others. I was born and raised in Bergenfield and still live there today, so it was easy to stumble in and out of The Circus back then. I miss the whole scene, except for one thing.

It was that horrible night in 1978 when it was a bar and restaurant called Peanuts, before it was Circus-Circus. I was there, right inside the door when it happened. I was maybe eight or 10 feet away when some guy pulled a gun from under his jacket and began firing. It was pandemonium. There were cops, ambulances, and more cops. In the days that followed, I would learn that a bouncer was killed and a patron wounded. The story I heard was that a customer was thrown out, because he was causing trouble and apparently drunk. That same customer stated that they hadn't seen the last of him. He followed through on his promise and returned with a gun. The rest was a nightmare.

LIZ DOBLER
MICHIGAN

There's probably more going on here in The Motor City than New Jersey and even Florida. I can't testify to it because I don't get out like I used to, but that's what I'm hearing from my fellow party mates.

I'm looking at a picture right now of Badlands at Circus-Circus in 1979, and I'm sure there are people I know in that crowd. Most of my friends were from Bergenfield, although I grew up in Teaneck. It was easy to get into the clubs underage. All you needed was a voter's registration card, and you could get into almost any bar you wanted to. I borrowed my friend's card and began my bar hopping days at sixteen. I remember going to Wally's in Bergenfield for almost two years and then turning 18, the legal age at that time. When they asked for my ID, I was goofy enough to give them my birth certificate. They looked at me in disbelief and said, get out of here.

When Crystal Ship played at Circus-Circus, there were always serious fights. Always serious fights! They brought in the rowdy crowd, but did a great cover for The Doors.

Any sex drugs and rock and roll stories?

All my friends smoked pot, but I wasn't a big pot head. I did my share of drinking back then; however, my time of partying was short lived. I remember going to Wally's with some friends and just drinking and drinking and drinking. We left there and went to Circus-Circus across the street to see what was going on. After a short time there, I left with this guy I had been seeing and went to a park in Teaneck to, I guess, make out. I got really tired and told him I wanted to leave. After working 70 hours that week and partying, I was exhausted. Needless to say, I fell asleep at the wheel on my way home that night and crashed my car into a tree on Liberty Road in Teaneck, right by The Armory. If you come across the blackened tree, that's the one I hit. That's my tree. I was messed up pretty bad, and my car was totaled. The year was 1981.

Back then, I worked hard and played hard. Now I just work hard and own my own flower shop in Waterford, Michigan just 45 minutes from Detroit. My interest in the flower business began when I worked in a flower shop in Dumont, New Jersey in between school and partying.

Given the opportunity all over again, I wouldn't miss it for the world. There's nothing like that anymore. The rules are so stringent on drinking and driving, I don't know how clubs even stay in business today.

KEITH McELWEE
NEW JERSEY

Many rock clubs existed in the 1980s offering an intimate live venue for up and coming musical acts and already established bands. Prior to the opening of the Meadowlands Arena in East Rutherford, New Jersey, you had to travel to the city or Long Island for a concert at a large theater or auditorium. Even the Capitol Theater in Passaic was a very formal venue.

Emerging on the scene was a new outlet for live bands to perform for their audiences. "Rock clubs" were popping up everywhere offering something different than your typical dance club or disco. At a rock club, you could hang at the bar, to the side, or in front of the stage where you could get into the music without actually dancing. At a dance club or disco, there were large unobstructed dance floors, which inferred that you either dance or stand against the wall like an ass hole, with the big L across your forehead.

Rock clubs were opening in New Jersey with multiple bars, outrageous sound systems, and amazing lighting effects, including clubs like Mother's, The Joint in the Woods in Parsippany, Circus-Circus in Bergenfield, and a host of others.

Name an event or memory that stands out from the club days?

One quick memory from Mother's. I still can remember a visit back to New Jersey from Miami, Florida in 1980, when the American hostages were taken in Iran. Mother's gave away bumper stickers when you entered that stated the opinion of the day; "Warning: I Don't Brake for Iranians."

Clubs up and down the Jersey shore coastline were demonstrating similar dissatisfaction of the crisis with shooting gallery games on the boardwalk depicting an image of the Ayatollah Khomeini being hit with paint balls. But my best recollection of the clubs up north was that they were always packed with people from all walks of life. Some leftover hippies, disco ducks, Jersey girls with big hair, but mostly rockers, looking for a night of memorable music and good times.

RENEE BANDAZIAN
NEW JERSEY

When I was 18 and 19 years old, my parents had a strict rule: I could go out any night of the week, if and only if, I made it to classes on time in the morning, maintained my grades, and worked my part-time job at Bamberger's.

So, my life in the very early 1980s revolved around a club somewhere four or five nights a week, following my favorite cover bands, with my friends Arlette or Judy or Donna.

Arlette and I loved the band E. Walker, for different reasons. I thought barefooted lead singer Ray was cute, and she thought the unsmiling keyboardist, Ace, had beautiful eyes and hair.

Depending on the night, I would be at The Soap Factory in Palisades Park, Creations in The Oranges, Mother's in Wayne, The Tow Path in West Paterson, Cuss from Hoe in Paramus, The Orangeburg Pub in Orangeburg, New York, and The Circus, of course.

I definitely went to The Circus (which my parents called "The Discotheque") one weeknight to hear a band. I can't remember who it was with any sense of certainty. Maybe Badlands? Rat Race Choir?

Dressed in my shiny teal Lycra spandex top, designer jeans, Candies stiletto mules (the only nod to the disco days), and white rabbit jacket, I gathered around the front of the dance floor, as a large cloud of cigarette smoke and bad perfume floated high above the floor all night. My mother could never understand how I reeked of cigarette smoke when I wasn't a smoker.

With my cousins generously refilling my glass with cranberry juice and vodka, (the precursor to the Cosmopolitan,) for free, I once actually got up on the stage with the band and played the tambourine! That was something I always wanted to do: be on stage with the band. The tambourine had been my only hope.

It was 2:45 am as it usually was, when I arrived home that night. Bleary eyed, I somehow made it to my 8 am class, and sat for a test. By lunchtime, I was sifting through the latest issue of The Aquarian to figure out that night's destination.

NORA CURRAN
NEW YORK

I must have gone to every bar that opened! There wasn't a place I didn't go! From New Jersey to Rockland County, New York, to Port Chester to Staten Island, Long Island, the Hamptons, you name it, I was there seven nights a week.

We went back and forth between the rock and disco scene. I liked disco, but rock and roll was easier to get in to. Rock and roll is a lot of fun! You could stand in front of a band, clap, and just get into it. With disco, you had to fit into a certain look or mold.

It was common practice to pile into a car (usually mine) because I was always the designated driver, then go to The Rusty Nail to kind of tune up on cheap drinks before paying higher prices at the hot clubs. Or maybe we'd go to 41 North in Porchester, where ladies could drink for 50 cents.

I guess you took advantage of ladies nights?

No doubt, it was great to be a woman back then. I knew every lady's night and every happy hour. You would strut up to the bar and say, "Give me an Alabama slammer or maybe a kamikaze. I'm going down!

I remember in another place you had to blow a whistle to get a shot. I didn't care, I just wanted the shot. It was a lot of fun. It was great.

I can still visualize The Archway on Gerome Avenue in the Bronx across the street from the funeral parlor. Oh my God! Everyone walked around with toilet paper stuck to their feet.

The best part of that era is that we had the greatest music of all time. There was something for everybody. The music never went through you, it "began" you. We were so lucky, we had everything! In my heart we had the best music of all time.

What's the worst part?

It's over!

ROSS DODWELL
NORTH CAROLINA

Hot cars, crowded smoky clubs, loud rock and roll music, and an abundance of great live bands. Was there ever a better time for live rock music? Sure, you could go see Led Zeppelin at Madison Square Garden along with 19,998 other crazy fans, or you could opt for one of the smaller clubs seemingly popping up all over New Jersey—all over the nation, in fact— like dandelions in the summer. When I think about that time period in my life, I think about clubs like The Stone Pony in Asbury Park, the Depot in Ramsey, and Circus-Circus on South Washington Avenue, in Bergenfield.

Here was the cool thing about The Circus—the front door was always locked. To enter, you needed to come in through the back door in the parking lot, show ID, and up a flight of stairs to arrive at the main entertainment room. I know that added to the mystique of the club. You could drive down South Washington Avenue, and completely miss the place, unless you were in the know.

We never worried about parking there, basically because most of the town of Bergenfield, closed down shortly after 6 pm, and all of the parking spots for neighboring businesses were up for grabs. Once the evening was underway, the place was wall-to-wall with people and as smoky as a forest fire. Didn't we all smoke back then?

It was the idea that you could see a major band like Steppenwolf, in a local club. They were so close you could reach out and touch them.

As I arrived at The Circus each night, lines began to form early. I waited as patiently as a 19 year old could, as the people at the door processed hundreds of club goers, checking IDs, in the short period of time required before each show time. Once in, it seemed as though the nights would never end.

It was a unique time period in American history that will sadly never happen again. I am glad to have had the opportunity to experience it firsthand, at my friend's club, Circus-Circus."

PAUL CENSULLO
NEW JERSEY

If you remember the TV series *Mission Impossible* with Jim Phelps played by actor Peter Graves, you'll also remember the theme song introducing each episode. As a 17 year-old Bergenfield High School student, Paul had his own mission every Thursday night, and it went like this.....

Once the lights were out and there was total silence, I made my move. Mom said good night and the house went dark. Cue the music...The theme song starts NOW! I slipped out of bed fully clothed, snuck across the hall and through my sister's bedroom window, and made it to the garage roof. From there I hung onto the gutter, jumped eight feet to the steps below, and then began sprinting to my destination; Circus-Circus.

It was the same routine every Thursday night, no matter what. Whether it was snowing, raining, or freezing cold, I wasn't going to miss my favorite band, Friends.

So how does someone underage get into a club?

My heart pounded every single time I went up that back staircase to enter the club. The question was always, will the bouncer my sister knows be at the door that night? Or, was I going to use my fake ID? Either way, I was getting in. Thursday nights were just electric. The Circus had the stage, the light show, and the big club feel. When I got home at 2 am, my ears were still ringing. I don't think I even heard my teachers in the first and second period. I couldn't wait for the next Thursday to come so I could do it all over again. There's nothing like seeing live entertainment.

My conversation with Paul quickly became somber when he spoke about his father's losing battle with cancer at just 48 years old, and how he dealt with it as a kid.

Going to clubs was an outlet for me. It was a place I could go and forget. It helped me to get through that whole process, and music will do that.

Music was such an influence on Paul that he went on to form his own band naming it TK Walker, which was a staple at Wally's every Wednesday night for years. Although his career path would change later, he originally went to college to be a music teacher.

It's part of my life. I'm still out there playing keys with a band called, Big Convention and enjoying every bit of it.

The Glamorous Life

The night ends. We're exhausted.

Everything, especially our clothes, smells like stale cigarettes and beer. Shoes stick to the deep red carpet, now a mixture of broken glass shards, paper wrappers, and cigarette butts. The dance floor hosts its own swampy bayou of broken glass and hundreds of empty or near empty beer bottles.

It's been a typical night, the only vagaries being: which bartender, bouncer, or waitress called in sick at the last minute? Whose drink wasn't strong enough or beer not cold enough? Which toilet clogged up and spilled its toxic load all over the bathroom floor? The list goes on and on.

But, it's closing time.

Up come the house lights. The DJ yells, "Let's go! Its hotel, motel, no tell, time!"

We lock the doors, my brother checks out the registers, and then we have a drink, then another, and another. We're exhausted but with enough energy to celebrate the night's success or complain about its failure. There was never a shortage of excuses if the night was a bust.

It was too hot!
Too cold!
Too dark outside.
It's summer and people are at the beach!
The band sucked and didn't have a following!
White Tiger's playing at Mother's and everyone went there!
It's too close to Arbor Day!
They predicted snow and everyone stayed home!

Alhough it seemed as if my evening would never end, my brother Jack's workday was always extended, and he never knew for how long. It was Jack's job to wait for the bands to break down the equipment and pack up. The speed of the roadies determined whether or not Jack would be home before sunrise.

Every night the routine was the same. My brother handed me the white bank sack with thousands of dollars in smelly wet cash, which I would deposit the next day. For security, Jack walks me to my shiny blue 1977 Cadillac. It's 3 am, and I'm starting to hear crickets. Add all the after-closing drinks to the four or five I downed during the evening, and I'm ready to drive home to Oakland, New Jersey, which is about a 35-minute ride. This is where the night becomes atypical. Somewhere near the River Edge, New Jersey border, I see flashing red lights in my rear view mirror. Hope I wasn't speeding. Maybe I have a tail light out? I pulled my car into a shopping center parking lot and waited for the inevitable "License and registration sir. Do you know why I pulled you over?"

"Not really," I said to the old cop, who was maybe in his forties. He told me I was swerving from lane to lane and asked where I was coming from and if I was drinking. I told him I had just closed the club, and yes, I was drinking.

"Where do you live?" he asked.

"Oakland," I responded.

"Well that's not too far, go slow. Do you want me to follow you?"

Can you imagine that happening today? Last week? I'm quite sure I'd have slept it all off in the comfort and care of the local police department, had this happened last night.

But by now it's 4 am I'm so wound-up I can't even think of sleeping. My wife and three year-old, Rick Jr., are sound asleep, so I tiptoe around quietly not to wake them. I grab a beer from the refrigerator; open the bank sack full of sticky bills, which by now smell like mold; and begin counting. Because we were depositing large amounts of cash, the bank wanted all the bills to face the same way. That kind of pissed me off, so I changed banks.

My new bank didn't care which way the money was facing. They just wanted it. On a good night it would take a half hour to an hour just to count and stack the money. And actually, money is probably the dirtiest thing any of us handled in a given day. Just imagine how many people in how many ways and how many places have touched your money. Still, I would rather be counting money than a lot of other things.

Now it's 10 am, and I'm back to the club for the lunch crowd. I pull into the rear lot and park in my usual spot. I began to walk up the first set of black metal stairs and notice the toilet paper on the ground that must have been stuck to someone's shoes. There is crap all over the place, literally. After a few more steps I see in plain view that the main floor is littered with the same beer bottles, spilled drinks, broken glass, and shit all over the place. Apparently, the maintenance crew hadn't shown up. After calling them and getting one excuse after the next, I wound up cleaning the place myself. The maintenance crew usually consisted of three or four people, but that morning, it was just me. By the time I was done cleaning puke from the floors, shit in the bathrooms, and broken beer bottles and glass, I was wrecked for the day, which had only just started.

It's cliché to say, but when you own a business, you own all of it—counting sticky money, vacuuming up broken glass, and cleaning up someone's puke.

The new maintenance crew started the next day. I stayed in upper management.

It's going to be a long night!

Gabba Gabba Hey:
The Ramones Come to New Jersey

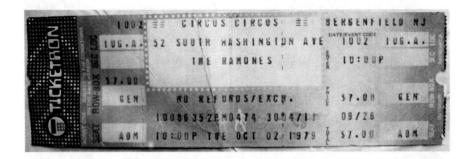

In dingy, sweaty venues from LA to New York, punk rock and new wave bands were re-telling the rock and roll story. In LA, it was X, the Blasters, the Germs, the Go-Go's, and the Knack. In Boston, it was the Cars and Human Sexual Response. In London, it was the Sex Pistols, Elvis Costello, the Jam, and the Clash.

In New York, it was Blondie, Talking Heads, and The Ramones.

So, it's a Wednesday night in the early autumn of 1979. We're packed. Condor, one of my favorite bands, is on stage, and my brother yells in my ear, "I just booked the Ramones!"

I'm like, "Who the hell are The Ramones?" I had never heard of them. The Revolution hadn't quite reached Bergenfield yet. But then again, I had never heard of The Police either.

A couple of weeks later, it's the early evening, tables are wiped down, glasses are washed, and we're getting ready for the sound check. The low hum of the PA oozes through the building.

Out of the maelstrom (actually, out of the parking lot) and into the club strolls the personification of the movement, "Commandanté Zero" of the Revolution—Joey Ramone.

He is the perfect combination of geek and cool. Six-feet-six in a worn black leather jacket and tattered jeans; his scraggly hair was falling over his thick, tinted John Lennon-style specs. He looks around. He looks at me.

Then, he speaks.

"Hey, man, got four quarters?"

I went to the cash register, gave him the quarters, and watched him move toward the pinball machines at the far end of the club.

Music-wise, the only thing I knew about The Ramones were the few songs I had heard on the tapes the promoters had given us. Nothing on those cassettes could have prepared me for the real thing.

At about 10:30 that night, Joey Ramone leaned forward and yelled into the mike, "We're the Ramones. Thank you, baby! One, two, three, four! One, two, three, four!"

Holy shit! It was like a 747 taking off, and Circus-Circus was the runway. They started playing at 150 miles an hour, maybe 200 miles an hour, nonstop. One song rolled into another and then another. This was fast and furious rock and roll, stripped down to its barest elements and cranked up to 12—hard driving, power chord rock and roll.

This was energy I'd never seen before, and I'd seen just about everyone. Just one Fender guitar, a Mosrite bass, a drummer, and a singer putting out huge, loud, white-hot sheets of sound. A small fortress of equipment pushed the driving music out to the furthest reaches of Bergen County—three Marshall heads running five 4 by 12 cabinets—three stage right, behind guitarist Johnny Ramone, and two stage left behind bassist Dee Dee Ramone, who was piloting two Ampeg SVT heads running two Ampeg 8 by 10 cabinets, one on either side of the drums. Suffice to say these are the most powerful stage amps in the business. Now, imagine all of those amps turned up all the way.

The audience members pogoed and bobbed their heads in hot, sweaty rock and roll delight. Even as their hair was blown back by the sheer volume of the music.

After several tunes played in quick succession with no introductions, no onstage patter, and barely any breathing, the sound and lights blew out somewhere in the middle of "Blitzkrieg Bop."

No problem. The PA and lights were restored, they restarted the song, and off they went, continuing their sonic assault.

In the middle of the tune "Rockaway Beach," it happened again. The show came to a screeching halt, like a silent train wreck. Dee Dee was pissed; so pissed that he took his white Fender Precision bass and slammed it against the wall of the stage with full force. Shiny, hot pieces of the guitar cascaded into the audience—much to their glee.

And that was the show.

Even in the halcyon days of the late 70s, The Ramones rarely got the recognition they deserved. They were never heard on most US radio stations. Recognition and membership in the Rock and Roll Hall of Fame came only much later.

Thirty years later, The Ramones' music actually sounds tame compared to a lot of new grindcore and death metal bands. And, tunes such as "Blitzkrieg Bop" and "Sheena is a Punk Rocker" are staples on Disney Radio. There's even a New York City street named after Joey Ramone, who passed away from cancer in April 2001.

My affection for the Ramones runs deep to this day. I still feel like a punk when I hear their music now, even though I might not have even qualified for the title back in the day.

For Christmas 2012, my sister bought me a book called *On the Road with the Ramones*. There, in the back of the book, is a long list of the dates, cities, and states where the band performed. They played about 250 dates a year in their heyday. Johnny Ramone kept a record of each and every gig.

On page 296, you'll see "October 2, 1979, Bergenfield, New Jersey." That was us. That was that night.

Whenever I go to a bar that plays live music, the first thing I do is ask the band to play a Ramones tune. And, of course, I brag that they once played at our club. The 20- or 30-something lead singer usually stares back at me vacantly, barely holding back from uttering, "Yeah, right, Gramps."

Guns and Poses

Atypical Thursday night. It's Ladies Night.

Before the law was changed as being unconstitutional, the ladies drank free for a couple of hours. Then, the band would crank out two sets. We saved the best for last—the bikini contest!

Summer Thursdays would rock, so before the doors opened, we had to be ready for 400 or 500 people. Bartenders Darren, Scott, and Big Tony would be behind the main bar cutting up fruit for drinks, setting out ash trays, and making sure their bar was stocked. Harry and Chet are doing the same at the two bars in the rear by the stage. Bouncers began their work shift at 9 pm, although we usually opened the doors at 8:30.

Unless we were hosting a concert or a major act was playing, there usually wasn't a line at that early hour. Even so, I knew that if there was any trouble, my brother, known lovingly as "Crazy Jack" in high school, would take care of it. And, certain bartenders would hop over the bar in a heartbeat if something went down.

It was typical back then that bartenders were male—until we hired Jill, a smoking-hot, reputedly former Jordache jeans model. She was tall, blonde, and very friendly to boot. Fifty guys could be lined up for a drink, and not one minded waiting 15 minutes for her—just so they could stare at her—even if the other bartenders were just wiping off the counter. (Like so many pretty girls, she appears in this anecdote as she did in the bar—lovely to look at, but not that germane to the story.)

On this particular Thursday night, the bartenders weren't wearing their usual Circus attire—company-issued red Circus shirt and black pants. Tonight was different. It was Ladies Night. Bartenders wore bright white tee-shirts, black bow ties, black pants, and wristbands. A great cover band was going to be playing that everyone loved (I can't say this was the case every night; it was a personal choice whether you liked the band), so we were pumped.

I'll be honest, I don't like deadhead music, but if there ever was a town that liked The Grateful Dead, it was Bergenfield. Did I love Timberwolf, the Grateful Dead tribute band? You bet I did! They packed the club every night they played.

It's precisely 8:30 pm and the imaginary bell sounds. Jack Sr. and Tommy the beer runner walk to the main entrance at the rear of the building and begin checking IDs and collecting the $3 cover charge until all the bouncers arrive. Customers are slowly coming up the two short flights of steps to get inside. Before they do, they're greeted with bright chaser lights racing around the "Circus-Circus New Jersey's Rock and Roll Emporium" sign at the first landing. For a lot of patrons, I'm sure just seeing those lights excited them—"We're almost inside!"

Side note: You're officially in the club at the top stair. The loud music instantly hits you in the face, and you lean into it. Meanwhile, the powerful woofers driven by DJ Tripp in the sound tower cause the floor to rumble under your feet. It was a powerful first impression, no matter how many times you visited the club.

Anyway, this Thursday, after the doors opened and in the first 20minutes or so, 10 or 15 customers arrived while I was moving about the club checking this and making sure of that.

Feeling relaxed about our readiness, I poured my first Tom Collins, lit up a smoke, and moved into the kitchen for some quiet time. My favorite seat in the house was the freezer chest; it was a cool, quiet spot to be by myself for a few minutes.

I was just starting to relax when I heard the double doors to the kitchen swing open with such force that I thought a tractor trailer was coming in. Bartender Darren rushed in looking like he had seen a ghost and obviously spooked he said, "There's a guy at the bar with a gun tucked in his pants. I just served him a beer."

Panic, adrenaline, and fear raced through my veins. My brother wasn't in the club at the time, and I didn't want my father involved; he tended to be a diplomat, and I frankly didn't want diplomacy.

You had to be an asshole to come into a bar, drink, and pack heat. I thought for a second that maybe he was a cop, but that couldn't be the explanation. Good way to lose your job, even in 1980.

We needed to handle this carefully.

I asked Darren to walk out of the kitchen with me and point the guy out. There weren't many people in the club at the time, and only a few were at the main bar; so it wasn't a problem getting a clear look at him from a short distance.

In one gradual and casual motion, I moved into his space, leaned forward against the bar, looked to my left, and then down to his waistband. I saw a pearl white handle of what appeared to be a small pistol. I looked twice from two different angles just to be certain, but there was no doubt.

I quickly made the decision not to bring in the police. They would've come in with guns blazing, and we didn't need the drama again. We had already had that scene a short time after our grand opening, and the memory of a bouncer being killed at Peanuts was still fresh in my mind.

I decided I was going to handle it my way. I enlisted two of our bouncers who had arrived early and keen-eyed Darren the bartender. I had Darren, the blonde heartthrob, Kurt at 6-feet-six, and Easy Al. Al was not the biggest bouncer in the place, but he was one of the toughest.

The plan was simple. When I gave the nod, Darren was to grab the guy's left arm, Easy would grab the right, and Kurt would put him in a head lock from behind. This would not allow him to move at all.

My job was to get the gun from his waistband. As more people started to gather at the bar, it became less obvious to the target that we were surrounding him and ready to pounce. With adrenalin pumping and sweat dripping down the sides of my thick mop of hair, I nodded and mouthed the word, "Now!"

Almost instantly, the thin, wiry customer was overpowered and pinned to the bar. During the brief scuffle, the bottle of Bud he had in front of him went airborne and landed behind the bar, soaking Big Tony.

Customer Zero is now locked in a frozen position. With only his legs free, he was trying to push back against the bar. "What the fuck is this?" I asked, pointing to the handle of the gun.

In a shaken and dazed state he stammered, "It's a cigarette lighter!"

Yeah, right.

I carefully lifted the white handle out of his pants and just stared at it in disbelief. Cigarette lighter it certainly was. I was so pissed I wanted to smash it in his face. "You're a real asshole, you know that?"

I still can't figure out why we didn't kick him out after the fiasco. Maybe it had something to do with the dozen or so apologies he gave us and the distinct relief that it wasn't all a lot worse.

Later on that night we finally threw him out for being a sloppy drunk.

I can't help but wonder how *he* tells this story.

It was a circus all right, and we never, ever ran out of clowns.

Twisted Sister: Who's Not Gonna Take it?

December 6, 1979. The chant begins.

Twisted Sister lead singer Dee Snider shouts out, "We are TWISTED!" The crowd yells, "FUCKING!" And Snider screams, "SISTER!"

Ah, the curious case of Twisted Sister.

On the one hand, this is a typical rock and roll story of suburban kids and snotty-nosed rebellion. At the same time, it's heavy-handed commercial pandering.

And kids loved it.

From The Factory in Staten Island to the Soap Factory in Palisades Park, Twisted Sister kicked ass wherever they went. No hit records yet, but they were still packing clubs all over the Northeast with their guys-dressed-like-girls-and rocking-like-bikers presentation.

I still remember my first impression of this band as if it were yesterday.

It was 10 pm Time for the first set.

Their manager was telling my brother that the group would be coming up from the dressing room shortly, and that he needed to get six bouncers ready for security. I went into the kitchen and eagerly waited for the band to emerge from the dressing room and climb the stairs to the stage.

I'd seen their faces on photos in *The Aquarian* but was curious to actually see them up close. After about five minutes, I heard the rumbling echo of loud footsteps coming from the stairwell.

The first head popped out through the door jamb revealing a tall—really tall—guy: lead singer Dee Snider, with a full face of colorful make up. It must have taken at least an hour to smear on. A bright pink women's outfit rested perfectly on his thin frame, complimented by his black nail polish and a shoulder draped with hanging chains. Thick, boot-like, high heeled platform shoes gave him an additional six inches in height, although it seemed like a lot more at the time. (None of these rock stars are very tall, as it turns out.) The other band members, similarly made up, followed behind Dee and waited for their manager to give the green light.

The club was packed, particularly in front of the dark stage. Wooden barricades were set up to separate the fans from the band, and only a small nightlight shined on the stage.

It was like the first few minutes before a Broadway musical opens.

Opening theme music blared from the double stack of Marshall amps, one on each side of the stage. Suddenly, the music stopped and the stage went pitch black. The crowd was screaming and stomping their feet calling for the band to come out. The whole building seemed to be quivering.

Three minutes went by and suddenly the band emerged from the kitchen to the stage, flanked by our bouncers. The band jumped onto the stage and assumed their positions.

The night began with Twisted Sister coming out swinging at full throttle with their famed opening introduction of "What You Don't Know." The stage was still dark for several seconds, and then the light show suddenly hit fans in the face. They were off. And the fans were off too!

It wasn't just the makeup, tight pants, and leather handed down from countless 70s rock/glam bands—from David Bowie to T-Rex to Mott the Hoople and then adapted by the new breed of 80s "big hair" bands. Instead, it was men dressed like women who wanted to make heavy metal rock. That was the basic idea. Add to that a smart-assed "I don't give a fuck" attitude, and you had Twisted Sister.

It was as if the loudest kid in your class decided the classroom wasn't big enough anymore. Dee Snider wanted to be the biggest brat anywhere. And, he was…kinda.

In fact, one national music magazine nailed it when it headlined a story on the band named "Twister Sister: Devils or Dorks?"

In the late 70s, disco was huge, and more than one young person was trading in a pair of faded jeans and a tee shirt for $80 Calvin Klein's and shiny polyester shirts. At the same time, rock and roll "traditionalists," if there is such a thing, were horrified by this trend and vowed to end this assault to the dance floor.

Twisted Sister saw themselves as leaders in the battle to stomp out disco in all its forms. They smashed disco records live on stage to encourage the movement, and some swear to this day that Twisted Sister had a hand in its demise, a demise that never really occurred.

They were in an odd space, time-wise, anyway.

In 1977, the soundtrack album to "Saturday Night Fever," a collection of disco hits, was the hottest selling album of the year. And Twisted Sister wouldn't actually have a hit record until 1984, with "We're not Gonna Take It."

In 1981, Twisted Sister was just filling up clubs all over the Northeast waiting for a bigger break.

Their show was half harangue, half hell set to music. They set up a nonstop conversation with the audience amidst the tunes, and no subject was off-limits.

Snider commented on current events. For example, in response to the November 4, 1979 takeover of the embassy in Tehran and the seizure of U.S. hostages they sang, "Bomb, Bomb, Bomb, Bomb, Bomb Iran. Bomb, Bomb, Bomb, Bomb, Bomb Iran!" to the tune of the Beach Boys' "Barbara Ann." It was a fairly obvious joke given the tenor of the times, but the audience ate it up with a spoon.

And, of course if you were standing down in front, or you were in their line of sight, you were open territory.

Nothing was off limits to Dee and Jay Jay French, the amazing lead guitarist for the group. They could embarrass even the most outgoing rocker.

Snider knew no boundaries, bellowing on stage that our club smelled like a circus, and that the place "sucked!" He promoted

Twisted Sister at Circus-Circus

the band's gigs, mentioning other clubs by name, which we had a policy against. If you tried to control him, though, he'd get worse.

My first reaction was to be pissed off. I was thinking, "I'm paying these guys to bash my club?" But my brother, who booked Twisted and all the bands, knew of their antics and told me to chill. It was all part of their show.

There is a famous story about The Who's Pete Townshend swinging his guitar around and getting it stuck in a club's low ceiling, thus initiating the band's legendary onstage destruction of their instruments. But this was not that historic moment.

Jay Jay French ended their set that night by sticking his guitar through my ceiling and walking away from the stage with the guitar just hanging there. I was like, now my ceiling is wrecked. What else are these guys going to do? Burn down the place?

Through the all-knowing eyes of hindsight, I've come to realize this band was a fascinating combination of brattiness and professionalism. When we first booked Twisted to play, they had their road manager inspect our facility a few weeks before the show to ensure that the gig would go smoothly. Among the laundry list of items that needed to be in place were things such as a clean dressing room, security, direct entrance for the band to the stage, (which we didn't have), and all the required voltage.

There was one significant hitch. The band's dressing room was only accessible through the kitchen, and a full flight of narrow metal stairs was the only way to get there. Each step to the basement had a one-inch space between the other. This was a problem for Twisted, because they wore platform shoes with high heels. I remember the road manager telling my brother that we needed to change our staircase for the show. That wasn't going to happen, so they agreed that we could tape up each step with electrical tape, thus eliminating the space between each step. This way, the boys wouldn't fall in their high heels. That would have spoiled their dramatic entrance for the evening.

I also remember asking Dee Snider if he wanted a drink before the gig. His response, "Thanks, I don't drink." I can't remember hearing that response once from any other band member. Of course, Twister Sister wasn't just any group. After all, drinking was the downfall of so many other great bands. Over the years, I've heard of and seen talented musicians being tossed out of bands, because they couldn't control a drinking or drug habit. Not this band, apparently.

Twisted Sister played at least three concerts at our club that I can recall. They played May 15, 1981, July 15, 1983, and a special WPLJ Night with DJ Jimmy Fink on January 30 1983.

Twisted Fucking Sister. Love them or hate them. They rocked every single night.

In my tireless effort to interview band members and others, I engaged the services of Dan Lorenzo, who at the time of this writing was the editor of *Steppin' Out* magazine. Dan's experience in interviewing legendary groups such as Kiss, Aerosmith, Slayer, Alice in Chains, and a host of others for the popular magazine, made him a perfect fit for this assignment. Not only has Dan conducted some very cool interviews for this book, (to which you'll see his name attached starting on the next page), but he was also, in two popular metal bands in the late 80s and 90s, which toured Europe and America. One such group, Hades, still tours on rare occasions and most recently performed at the 'Bang Your Head' festival in 2010 as the opener for Twisted Sister, Queensryche, and Nevermore in Germany.

AN EXCLUSIVE INTERVIEW WITH **TWISTED SISTER'S JAY JAY FRENCH** AND THEIR NOT SO TWISTED ATTITUDE! INTERVIEW BY DAN LORENZO

If there was one bar band that stood head and shoulders above all the others with their sights set on fame and fortune, it was Twisted Sister. Twisted Sister was no stranger to the New Jersey club scene long before Circus-Circus ever opened.

Guitarist Jay Jay French told me, "When you worked a room in Jersey, you worked for five or six nights straight. You would basically do a residency in one room in 1973 or 1974. In those days a starting band could make $150 per night, and by earning as little as $900 per week, you could run a profitable business. You could make a living because gas was 29 cents per gallon and hotels were about $19.95 per night at the local Red Roof Inn. You could play somewhere off the Jersey Turnpike and just stay there for a week. The band would all stay in one room. You could make a profit because your expenses were so low. That was the classic Jersey scene. It was five, 40 minute sets. You started at 9 pm. On weekends you'd start at 10. You'd finish at about 3 or so in the morning. I was 22, so I guess I wasn't sleeping much.

"In 1979 it was a very different thing. The clubs in New Jersey like The Soap Factory, The Hole in the Wall, Mother's in Wayne held a lot of people. Circus-Circus in terms of size was the smallest club we played. I remember having to walk up fire escapes to get to the dressing room, which was really strange."

I asked Jay Jay if he envisioned Twisted Sister becoming even more popular after they'd already become the biggest bar band in the Tri-State area. He said, "We operated on two separate tracks. One was to become the biggest bar band, and the other track was to become famous worldwide. I always tell people, 'Before you can be The Beatles you'd better be better than the band next door.' It was a really big competition between us and all the other bands. It was us and Rat Race Choir, White Tiger, and Crystal Ship. We were very predatory, so we had to blow these other bands away. It became a contest. Can we outdraw these other bands? The king of all the clubs was The Fountain Casino. We broke the record there when we drew 4,900 people on a Monday night. We had heard White Tiger did 3,900 or something like that, so we were out to beat their number. It became very much a contest. The drinking age was 18, and the clubs were so massive that you actually played to more people than most concert bands did."

I often found myself in the audience to witness the Twisted spectacle in those days and remember what an honor it was for me when my band, Hades (which was a cover band in 1982), got to open for Twisted Sister at The Soap Factory in Palisades Park. Twisted Sister had released a couple of 45s at that time and then a self-financed EP. I envisioned the members of Twisted Sister partaking in wild groupie sex and earning and spending a fortune.

Jay Jay told me, "I never thought it was going to last forever, and I never spent any money. We spent every dollar we ever made on demos and making the band bigger. We had a very strict policy on salary. We kept it very low to reinvest all the money all the time. I thought we'd have a ten-year run. When the drinking age went up [to 21] it was apparent that we were on an iceberg that was melting. We refused to live an extravagant lifestyle."

Fair enough. At least Jay Jay must have some wild groupie stories to share with me...right?

"I have to tell you the band was all business 100% of the time. That's maybe the biggest misconception...the party side. We never did. It was never a goal. There was no sex, no drugs, no alcohol, no nothing. It was 100% work. What everybody did groupie wise was their business, because we never talked about it. I don't know if other bands sat around in the dressing room comparing notes, but we never did. It was a personal thing."

Twisted Sister left the cover scene behind and went on to international success and was, for a time, an MTV staple. The group's popularity waned, and they called it a day in 1988.

The band re-united after 9/11 and remains a very large concert draw particularly in the European festival scene. Twenty-eight years after my band Hades opened for Twisted Sister at The Soap Factory, we once again shared the stage with Twisted Sister at the Bang Your Head Festival in Germany in 2010. Twisted headlined. Thirty-thousand heavy metal fans got to relive the Twisted Fucking Sister experience.

So, how does Jay Jay make a living nowadays? Managing Twisted Sister! The band still, to this day, rakes in a small fortune thanks to commercials that feature the hits We're Not Gonna Take It and I Wanna Rock. There are re-releases and European festivals in dozens of countries that get to taste what it was like in the New Jersey club scene decades ago.

Ever the perfectionist, Jay Jay wanted to be sure everybody knew this,

"What the 10 years and 6,000 + performances in the bars did was teach us extreme performance discipline, which is still evident to this day. We still get to all venues 3 to 4 hours ahead of time. We eat, do a sound check, where possible, and then mentally prepare for each show. Dee does 90 minutes of vocalizing every night. We always get to the stage at the contracted time, every night. We never take the audience for granted. We never keep the audience waiting like some very big and very stupid bands do. We always play all the hits and all the songs that the fans want to hear. We play them exactly like the record, because that's what the fans really want. We are professional entertainers who now play to an average crowd of 50,000 fans at each show. These are the lessons that we will take to our graves courtesy of everything we learned playing places like Circus-Circus."

Circus-Circus Memorabilia

Circus-Circus Memorabilia

No Crime Here! Just Nursery Cryme

There are tribute bands, and then there are *tribute bands*. If you weren't looking directly at the stage and its performers, you would think that Peter and Phil were in the house. Rockers made their way from every corner of the Tri-State region to see a group that sounded just like Genesis. Let me rephrase that. They looked, sounded, and moved like that famous English rock group, except they were the ever-so-popular tribute band, Nursery Cryme. They packed clubs and entertained Genesis fans wherever they played.

Whether a cover band, tribute band, or solo performer, every act has its history and endless war stories of humble beginnings. Front man Bruce Martin and his tribute band Nursery Cryme were no exception.

My brother Jack reminisced about his history managing the band and taking them from block dances, backyards, and birthday parties to big time clubs and big time crowds. "As a sophomore at Glen Rock high school, I would try and go to every dance the school sponsored with my good friend Doug Carter, including one on a cold November night in 1975. After consuming a six pack, we stumbled into the party and wound up at front stage watching a band called, The Light, which played the music of Led Zeppelin, The Who, The Beatles, and other cool stuff. I remember these guys being old, very old. Maybe 20 or 21," recalled Jack. "Being only 15, anyone who could buy beer legally was old to me," he said.

"As the night wound down, we hung around to bull shit with the band. After a short time and some small talk, I had learned that the band consisted of Glen Rock High School graduates from five years prior, including Bruce Martin. Doug and I continued with some small talk and asked where they would be playing next. There was total silence," he remembered.

"We left that night and headed home to get a few hours' sleep before Doug and I were expected at my family's diner business at sunrise. I was the short-order cook on weekends, and Doug, who we fondly nicknamed 'Jaws' because he gladly ate all the mistakes, was my helper. Between poached eggs and pancakes with eggs over-light (which almost made me puke from a hangover), we kind of figured out together that with all the Glen Rock weekend keg parties going on, maybe we could book The Light at some of them".

"We approached Bruce with the idea, and soon it became one gig after another. From garages to basements to driveways, they played anywhere. Of course the parents were away, so I'm sure they wouldn't have minded that some of the living and dining room furniture had to be temporarily relocated to the rear yard. The band didn't expect to be paid a lot of money, but we did pass around a hat, while reminding the crowd that Bruce was old enough to buy beer, which was a motivator in itself. The later it got, the better the band sounded. Not that it had anything to do with the booze and weed! The length of each party usually depended on when the cops arrived. Sometimes they couldn't even get through a set, and others went on all night. The band and the property owner's kid usually had to deal with the police, which usually resulted in just a warning. Could you imagine if we were doing this today? You and your parents would be arrested, your mug shot would be in every local newspaper, and your lawyer would be telling you he may be able to get you off with a suspended sentence, provided you pay a fine and did 300 hours of community service," he joked.

"Everyone was happy. The band got exposure, the kids had fun, and every once in a while someone got laid, and they couldn't wait to brag about it at school. The party lasted all through my high school years, and then Bruce and I lost touch. At least that was the case until The Circus".

"Now, you've got to know where Bruce is coming from. The Martins were a very musical family with many players and pickers among them. His mother, in fact, had been a professional opera singer. Music was not just a hobby for Bruce. Music moved Bruce. He channeled it. He loved it. And he lived it. You could easily see by the ecstatic look on his face as he played, that it was truly his soul," Jack remembered.

"It was probably sometime in 1981 when a band that I had booked to play the club crapped out on me. A light bulb went off in my head, and I thought of Bruce's band, The Light. (no pun intended). After reaching out to him, I found that the band no longer played together, but Bruce had another idea. He suggested I hire him to do a solo act playing guitar and singing," he remembered. "Bruce, get your ass over here! That's all I remember saying. With no time to prepare even a set list, Bruce showed up an hour later with guitar in hand, a harmonica in his shirt pocket, and a lot of confidence. He went on stage that night and performed in front of a relatively small crowd but played with the energy and passion as though he were playing Madison Square Garden".

"His gigs continued for several months on and off before I received a call from Bruce asking me to check out a new band he put together called, Nursery Cryme."

"The band played tribute to rock group Genesis with the name borrowed from their album, Nursery Cryme, which was released in 1971. It was the group's first album with drummer Phil Collins and guitarist Steve Hackett".

"On any given Sunday, I would bring in and audition new bands that may have given me a demo tape that I thought were worth a look. Most sounded nothing like the tape, but there was always hidden talent that you just had to dig for, which meant going through a dozen just to find one. You might say I was the original Simon Cowell…That was awful…Next!"

Jack went on to audition Bruce's new tribute band. According to their drummer Jay Dittamo, the original members were Tony Raber on keyboards (later replaced by Dave Ross), David Hess on guitar, Jay on drums, Randy Dembo on bass, and vocalist Bruce Martin.

"They went on stage and just blew me away...I mean they were great! As they played 'Follow You Follow Me' my mind started to drift as I began to imagine just how good they could be with a little tweaking. I visualized a real sound system...I'm talking Marshall amps stacked to the ceiling, a lighting show worthy of a national act, a smoke machine to fill the deck with special effects, and all the stuff that goes with creating a rock band that you could take on the road and fill clubs. Add to the mix the proper marketing with radio, print advertising, tee shirts, etc. I knew these guys could get into the big clubs. I'm talking 1,000 and 2,000 capacity rooms."

Fast forward....

Jack went on to manage the group and everyone was happy at the beginning. All of the above actually did happen, right down to the smoke machine. But, just like every start-up company, it came at a price and much sacrifice.

"With the band well-rehearsed and every detail down to the stage wardrobe perfected, we were ready to rock. In just two visits to the recording studio, we nailed it down so tight that you'd believe you were listening to Genesis on the tape. It was THAT good, because I remember having to place a disclaimer in the radio spots stating, 'This is not Genesis you're listening to, This is Nursery Cryme'" he said.

"With resources available to me from the club operation, I was able to bring on a professional sound and light company to tour with the group at a favorable rate, and then convinced a top booking agent, Kevin Brenner, who was booking Twisted Sister and several other top flight bands at the time, to take on the group and book gigs for us. Back then and maybe even today, you had to be aligned with a reputable agency if you wanted to play the biggest and best clubs. A contract between the band and the club had to be signed for each gig. It was the real deal! No agency! No contract! No gig!"

The band went on to achieve great success and played at top venues in front of large crowds such as Hammerheads in Long Island, The Hole in the Wall in Rochelle Park, The Rock Palace in Staten Island, Mother's in Wayne, and many others.

But bands, just like marriages, break up half the time. Ask The Eagles, The Beatles, Pink Floyd, Van Halen...should I go on? And nasty lawsuits followed most of the time. There are a million reasons why they do, but it's never his or her fault.

Jack continued, "Well, our band was no different, and the disputes began to escalate. Our timing wasn't perfect coming out in the early 80s, although we had what many would call a good run, even though short-lived. The drinking age would soon increase, cutting the clubs' business in half, and no longer did the clubs have the income to pay the bands what they were used to. The problem, which wasn't unique to Nursery Cryme, was that we had a large infrastructure to feed, and the income wasn't there any longer. When that happens, people start to point fingers and the marriage goes sour."

The band did go on to play together on and off until around 1998 with several personnel changes. Of course the days of playing in front of crowds of 1,000 or more were gone, but the memories are still intact.

With a heavy heart Jack spoke about Bruce Martin's passing on June 13, 2008.

"He was way too young and way too full of life. I don't have many regrets in my life, but there are two that come to mind when I think of Bruce. I'm sorry I never told him how much his friendship meant to me and just how much I really enjoyed the Nursery Cryme experience. Undoubtedly, Nursery Cryme was Bruce's 15 minutes of fame, and he deserved that and so much more."

THE ALL NEW! **Circus, Circus**

APRIL 1980

52 S. Washington Avenue, Bergenfield, New Jersey
Plenty Of Parking

(201) 385-6604

Sunday	Monday	Tuesday	Wednesday	Thursday	Friday	Saturday
CLOSED	CLOSED	1 THE BADLAND BAND *Free Admission*	2 N.J.'s #1 Party Band FRIENDS	3 COURTNEY	4	5 IMPACT
6	7	8 THE BADLAND BAND *Free Admission*	9 FRIENDS	10 COURTNEY	11	12 RAT RACE CHOIR
13	14	15 THE BADLAND BAND *Free Admission*	16 FRIENDS	17 COURTNEY	18	19 TRIGGER
20	21	22 THE BADLAND BAND *Free Admission*	23 FRIENDS	24 COURTNEY	25 COURTNEY	26 SPECIAL CONCERT
27	28	29 THE BADLAND BAND *Free Admission*	30 FRIENDS			

N.J.s Rock & Roll Big Top 385-6604

CIRCUS CIRCUS

1st ANNUAL FESTIVAL OF BANDS

6 Of N.J.s' BEST BANDS IN CONCERT

Starts at 3 P.M. Sunday June 1st 1980

CRYSTAL SHIP
Trigger
DESPERATE MEN
Taxi
BAD LAND BAND
FRIENDS

Admission $4 Per Person
★ *52 South Washington Ave. Bergenfield N.J. (Plenty Of Parking)* ★

Give Our Regards to Broadway

In 1980, we were untouchable. Everywhere we turned was the right road. We didn't seek out publicity; the publicity Gods just picked up the phone and called us. Let me describe one Friday afternoon. I was moving in and out of the kitchen checking on the lunch business, when a waitress told me I had a phone call. I made my way to the office and heard a voice on the other end telling me he was with a production company in New York City.

Can we meet? Of course we can!

I set up an appointment with a guy named Anthony, and we met at the club a few days later. I hoped for a minute that they wanted to use our club to shoot a movie scene or something, but we weren't *that* lucky. The film company was looking for a place to conduct all-day interviews for "fresh faces" for an upcoming movie called *Times Square* starring Tim Curry. You know him as Dr. Frank N. Furter from the iconic *Rocky Horror Picture Show*. The film would also need extras to play punk rockers running through Times Square in midtown Manhattan.

It didn't take more than two minutes for me to agree. After all, it was more free publicity (my favorite thing), and they needed a place big enough to accommodate the anticipated large crowd.

Within a couple of weeks, the ads began running in several area newspapers. The film company conducted interviews at Circus-Circus for an upcoming movie, and they were looking for new faces.

Momentum began to build, and the phones began to ring nonstop. The interviews would be on a first-come, first-served basis at the club, beginning at 9 am on that Saturday. I didn't know what to expect. This was all new to me.

After a busy Friday night with 600 guests, three fights, and some blood on the dance floor, I returned to my home at 4 am. After a few hours' sleep, still totally exhausted, I dressed and headed back to the club.

The morning air was cool and foggy. I couldn't see 100 yards in front of me. After the usual 35 minute ride from my home, I approached the rear parking lot. I couldn't believe what I saw next. There were hundreds of kids wrapped around the building, and it was only 8 am, one hour before the doors were supposed to open. Young teenagers, many with their moms and dads in tow, brightened the cloudy morning with their colorful punk outfits and crazy hairdos.

When I unlocked the door, it was as though I held the key to the Willy Wonka Factory. Imagine all of them yelling and screaming and scheming to get inside. Minutes later, my sisters Lori and Michele (13 and 15 years of age) showed up with my mother and were almost attacked by the mob, with many complaining, of course, about why they were allowed in when no one else was.

The production crew showed up a short time later, and they were excited at the turnout.

At about 9:15 am we unlocked the doors and began allowing the wannabes to enter in a single line. I could see in the faces of the young, happy crowd that they wanted to please the interviewer in any way they could. Although my two sisters initially had no intention of being considered, they agreed to interview after some friendly encouragement from my mother.

When all was said and done, the film staff took names, phone numbers, and addresses of their potential candidates. The next step was to wait and hope for "the call."

I don't know what really happened after that but I know my sister Lori was called and asked to be an extra for the movie. She would be dressed as a punk rocker running through Times Square with the rebellious crowd, yelling and screaming. My poor mother had to wait all night for her to finish. Times Square in 1980 was not the Disneyland it is now.

I think Lori was paid $100 for the night—about $304.00 in 2014 dollars. Not a bad wage for a teenaged kid to stay out all night in New York City—and be in a rock and roll movie.

I'm sure you can find the film on any number of online movie sites. The sound track for the movie has lots of great punk rock and new wave music and is a real snapshot of the time; at least as filtered through the Hollywood eye. What's even better is that two of the greats that rocked Circus-Circus, The Ramones and David Johansen, are on the sound track.

Oh, and look for Lori in the Times Square riot scene! She's the one dressed like a punk rocker.

Rock N' Roll
Emporium

Circus, Circus

Ladies & Gentlemen In The Center Ring...

Every Tues
BAD LAND BAND
Free Admission

Every Wed
PEGASUS
Free Admission Before 10 p.m.

Thurs Feb 28
CRYSTAL SHIP
Renaissance Of The Doors

Fri & Sat Feb 29 & March 1
The Triumphant Return Of
CONDOR

Every Sun & Mon In March
CLOSED

Fri & Sat March 7 & 8
N.J.'s #1 Party Band
FRIENDS

52 S. Washington Ave., Bergenfield, N.J.
(201) 385-6604—Plenty Of Parking

I Fought the Law, and the Law Won

D id I happen to mention anywhere so far in these pages how great we were doing? I'm sure I've said it here somewhere, but have I touched on the lines out the door every night, the great bands, the rocking reputation, and the magic touch that seemed to follow our every move when it came to Circus-Circus?

Did I mention that I am the same bonehead who agreed that it would be a great idea to name our nightclub in Jersey after a world-renowned, circus-themed hotel and casino in Las Vegas, Nevada?

Yes, it actually occurred to me that no one would ever make the connection, that no one would ever see any resemblance between the two, and most importantly, that it wouldn't matter if anyone saw it. I'm half-genius, but half-genius might also be half-stupid.

There we were, the three of us, double-parked in a handicapped space, sitting on top of the world, with nothing to do all day and all night but stock the beer, book the bands, pour the drinks, and collect the money.

And then one day…As if summoned from on high, we received a letter in the mail from none other than the deep-pocketed, CircusCircus Hotels, Inc. threatening us with a lawsuit for trade name infringement. The letter came from the esteemed law firm of Mason Fenwick and Lawrence, of Washington, D.C. When I saw the letter, I said to my father, "They're fucking kidding us, right?" Here we were, little guys from New Jersey being threatened by a big time player in Vegas. When my father originally suggested we name our club Circus-Circus after the casino, I thought nothing of it at the time. Um, silly me.

I soon came to realize that in the casino world, there are no little guys. You're a mark, whether you're strolling through the casino lobby, or you're 4,000 miles away in New Jersey, and the house always wins.

My first reaction was to fight, but then I realized that even selling all the beer in the Tri-State area couldn't begin to finance a fight against these guys. Not to mention the fact that, well, they thought of the name first. We thought of the name second, just after we heard the name of *their* place. Can you see where this is going?

On January 1, 1981, as a compromise (another word for complete and total capitulation), we agreed to change our name to The Circus, which the hotel/casino lawyers graciously agreed was okay. Everything had to go. Everything had to be changed—signs, stationery, logo, tee-shirts, even the backstage passes. But having the name Circus-Circus for almost 21 months did put us on the map.

But I wonder. Had we bought the same building with the same bars, hired the same staff and the same bands, created the same exciting atmosphere, and called it "Jumping Jacks" or "Al's Rock Palace," or even the "Rock and Roll Heaven," would we have been just as successful? We'll never know.

For the longest time I tried to figure out how we got busted for the name infringement. The rumor was that a senior manager at the Vegas casino saw a tee-shirt bearing the name Circus-Circus from Bergenfield, New Jersey. The news quickly went up their food chain. The rest is history.

And even though they say the winners write history, I found a way to capitalize on the battle.

Like a true club owner, I called every radio station and newspaper to tell them Circus-Circus Hotels, Inc. in Las Vegas was suing us. Here was a tailor-made story: "Little Club Sued by International Casino! A Nation Gasps!" It made for great PR, which I could track like a drug-sniffing dog at Newark Airport. WPLJ radio called me live on the air about 6 or 7 am one morning. They called the story "The Long Arm of the Law." All I could think was that if Circus Circus in Vegas has our little club on its radar, we must be doing something right. Or we were doing something perfectly wrong, which was good too.

The story also appeared in several local newspapers. Our customers sat at the bar buzzing for weeks about the potential lawsuit. We were only too happy to assuage their thirst, their fears, and their curiosity.

Drink up kids, the law is coming down.

LAW OFFICES
Gelman and Gelman

FABIAN BUILDING
45 CHURCH STREET
PATERSON, N.J. 07505

523-8050
AREA CODE 201

November 17, 1980

Mr. Jack Bandazian
90 Woodvale Road
Glen Rock, N.J. 07452

Re: Circus Circus

Dear Jack:

Two months ago we sent a letter to the Washington D.C. law firm representing Circus Circus Hotels, Inc., regarding their claim against your company for trade name infringement. At that time we indicated that we would discuss the matter with you and get back to them shortly. We have never gotten back to them nor have they communicated again with us. Shall we let a sleeping dog lie? The choice is yours.

Very truly yours,

GELMAN AND GELMAN

By _____
Barry A. Cohen

BAC/idp

Nov 17 4:35 PM - would you believe - after dictating letter, that atty called: Please call me to discuss - now he's pressing!
Bar

Gelman and Gelman

November 20, 1980

Mason, Fenwick & Lawrence
310 OFC Building
1730 Rhode Island Ave., N.W.
Washington, D.C. 20036

ATTENTION: Boynton P. Livingston, Esq.

Re: Circus Circus Hotels, Inc.
Our client - Circus Circus
Bergenfield, N.J.

Dear Mr. Livingston:

We conferred against with our client who has agreed to discontinue the use of the
name "Circus Circus". Our client will, as of January 1, 1981, conduct business as
"The Circus". Our State registration will be revised.

The 1981 telephone directory can not be corrected at this time. As of the 1982
directory, the listing will be revised.

All of our client's exterior signs will be replaced as soon as possible, but no later
than April, 1, 1981. Our client conducts a small business and cannot afford to purchase all new signs immediately. After the Holiday seasons, new signs will be ordered.

Very truly yours

GELMAN AND GELMAN

By_____
Barry A. Cohen

BAC/idp
Copy to: Mr. Jack Bandazian

It's our Grand Opening! Again!

Forty days. We had just 40 days to reinvent ourselves as The Circus, which we agreed to do to avoid a major lawsuit. We'd poured a tent full of money into radio spots and other media promoting Circus-Circus. Now we were trying to reinvent ourselves in just over a month.

Our "hurry, hurry, hurry, to Circus-Circus" jingle was so popular and ran so often on primetime New York radio stations that today people still remember it and repeat it. And now we were gonna change it to "hurry, hurry, hurry, to The Circus?" Could we pull this off?

We already lost the 18 -year old drinkers. The drinking age was up to 19 and things seemed to be slowing down a bit.

A new look, a new jingle, and an increase in legal capacity was the direction we decided to take, especially if we wanted to grow our concert crowd. It had to happen fast, and there was no looking back. After nearly two years of success, we had the money to plow back in. But this time, it was going to be done right—not like the bare-bones shoe string budget we had when we first opened. I wanted the renovations to be well-planned and done quickly.

We had to close but for how long? With the doors shuttered, there would be no cash coming in for a while. Our competition might also grab our market share, even if it was for just a few weeks. Maybe they would grab a good bartender or other valuable employee of ours.

We hired an architect and contractor with the stipulation that the job be complete in record time. Three new bars needed to be built, the kitchen would be reduced to one-third its original size, and a fire escape was needed in order to safely increase the legal capacity.

The stage would be larger, and we would make The Circus theme a more pronounced part of the club. The original large rectangular bar in the front room was now a 50-foot long straight run down the wall.

Once we had opened up the floor space, reduced the kitchen size, and built the additional fire exit, we had 30% more capacity—that's another 150 people drinking.

For three weeks, it was day and night hammers, nails, buzz saws, and dust. I can still smell the new red carpeting and the fresh-cut wood as the job neared completion. We accented the ceiling with special effects lighting—chaser and strobe lighting would be operated from the DJ booth. Colorful roaming lights would wander throughout the club as the music blared between sets. Things were beginning to look bright and shiny. But how long would it last?

We were about to become The Circus. Radio spots were ready to go and ads were already running in *The Aquarian Weekly*. The phones began to ring nonstop, with everyone wanting to know when we would re-open and who would open the new place.

Our Friday 8 pm opening arrived in a blink. The team of bartenders, bouncers, waitresses, and beer runners began trickling in through the door. The vibe was palpable. "It's good to be back, and I'm proud to say I work here!" This made perfect sense. We were all in our twenties, working in a popular rock club, listening to the best bands in the area, and checking out a lot—and I mean a lot—of the opposite sex.

I mean, would you even talk about your job if you worked at Alexander's in Paramus, New Jersey?

Obviously, it was important for the new grand opening to be a success. The place needed to be packed, and we needed a great band. After pulling a few strings on short notice, we were able to hire Crystal Ship, the premier Doors tribute band.

I think the band may actually have bumped another club to give us both Friday and Saturday nights. My brother Jack's friendship with the band's lead vocalist, Joe Tag, probably didn't hurt either. The two had become such good friends that Jack went on to become the best man in Joe's wedding to his wife Donna. They were really tight.

Joe looked, sounded, and had the stage theatrics of Jim Morrison. If you closed your eyes, you would think it was The Doors. Every band member played exceptionally well, and they faithfully duplicated the legendary group's sound.

Joe founded the group in 1978 after attending the University of South Carolina on a football scholarship. He went on to study music, poetry, and philosophy. Does that sound like anyone you knew in college?

How good were they? Good enough and confident enough to rent The Capital Theatre in Passaic, New Jersey and not be surprised when 3,000 enthusiastic fans showed up. A feat that few, if any, other club bands could equal.

As The Capital Theatre program states, "Rarely in the nine years or so of the Capital Theatre's existence as a premier rock venue has a group without a recording contract played here. Crystal Ship's appearance marks one of those infrequent instances. The rock quintet is exceptional in a number of different ways."

There were certain bands that drew what we called "the drinking crowd," while others attracted people who drank less. Country rock bands drew customers who were known to drink more beer than liquor, and a party band such as Friends would bring a crowd that drank more mixed drinks. Crystal Ship brought in both a drinking and a rowdy crowd. How could they not?

There are certain songs that seem to fire-up a crowd. I'll give you three examples: "Roadhouse Blues," "L.A. Woman," and "Break on Through." Need I say more? There's no better way to ignite a crowd than the music of The Doors, especially when it's played perfectly, note for note. Visualize this. The band is playing and the crowd is causing the dance floor to rumble like a small earth quake. Add four or five beers, some weed, and you're in 20-year-old nirvana.

So, Crystal Ship was the perfect choice, and the weekend was magical. Nine hundred people came through the doors on Friday night and 1,100 more came on Saturday. Legal capacity was 600 to 700. You do the math. Anyway, it was a huge success.

Crystal Ship had a long successful run, but not without tragedy. Keyboard player Mark Zeborowski drowned in a freak accident on Halloween Eve while celebrating the holiday with friends on a party boat. Mark was not only a talented musician, but also one of the nicest guys you'd ever meet. I was sick when I heard about it. And then on March 29, 2009, lead vocalist Joe Tag passed away, most likely from the weight of his life, which he lived at full speed. Ironically, he lived as Jim Morrison might have lived, had Morrison lived longer.

You can ask most baby boomers in the Tri-State area about Crystal Ship, and they'll tell you that they've either seen or heard of them. They'll probably also tell you that they were at the grand opening or the new grand opening.

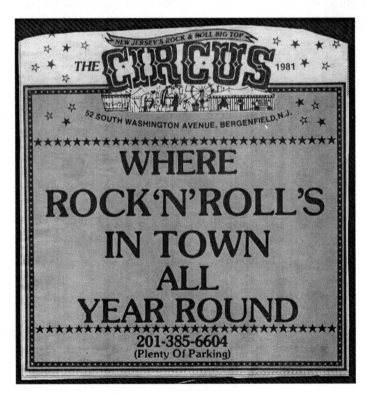

The all new Circus

Bouncers and Bouncing

In a competitive industry like nightclubs, nothing surprised me, and no rumor was too strange. I'd actually heard that one of our competitors sent in their bouncers during our opening week to start fights. Fights in the club meant that girls would be turned off and not return. No girls meant no guys and thus no business.

Whether we knew it was a competing club's bouncers or not, troublemakers found the exit doors pretty quickly, mostly via the air route. The word soon got out: fool around at Circus-Circus, and you're going down the stairs head first.

Locating the right bouncer was part art, part science, and part muscle. But the first place we looked was right on the dance floor. When a 6-foot-5-inch male customer came in, perhaps a college athlete or one who looked like a college athlete, I would sooner than later approach and ask if they'd be interested in bouncing. Explaining our expectations, I would make it very clear to them: "It's not your job to go around beating up people. You're there to prevent fights, not start them."

I made the mistake a few times of hiring bouncers who thought they were there to think with their fists. They didn't last. And, when the time came to tell them they were done, we gave the job to the toughest guy in the place—my young brother Jack. No one argued with him.

In addition to the eight to 12 bouncers we had on a busy night (we liked to keep a ratio of one bouncer per 50 to 75 customers), there was the thankless job of "beer runner." Think of it as a rock and roll coal miner, lugging heavy loads across an ever-increasing distance all night long. The runner's basic job was to keep the coolers filled with beer at three bars, navigate heavy cases of beer up stairs and through large, exuberant crowds. The walk-in cooler was at the far end of the basement (yes, downstairs,).

On a busy night, a beer runner was carrying some 100 to 150 cases up from the basement to keep the thirsty crowds sated. Of course, the distance from the cooler to the bars only got longer as the night wore on. So, by the end of the evening, a beer runner was a Sherpa tackling the Himalayas, and the mountains kept growing.

Getting back to the bouncers. They kept law and order sometimes by mere intimidation and other times by force when necessary. I always hoped it would be accomplished by intimidation.

If you are a naïve optimist, you'd better not run a rock club. There was always someone or a group that wanted to test us to see how far they could push the envelope of bad behavior. At least a few nights every week and just for fun, someone would rip out a sink, usually in the men's room or punch holes in the walls until we lined them with a nondestructive material. Two poor souls got caught by my brother one evening, and I'm certain they'll never forget it. He beat the living shit out of both of them. Thank God there weren't cell phones in those days, or it would have definitely made *I Witness News*. The punishment was so bad that the guys who did the damage actually called the police rather than the other way around. What is testament to the changing times is that they actually came back in the club the next afternoon, took responsibility, and paid us for the damage. Most important to them was that they were allowed back in the club. Today, everyone has their attorney on speed dial.

A bouncer working at a club, any club, knows intuitively when a fight either starts or is about to start. If you have ever worked security, you know exactly what I'm talking about. This is the same sixth sense that dogs have; super hearing and a response time seconds ahead of any human. It goes like this. You're sitting in your living room watching TV on the couch with your dog. His head abruptly comes off your lap and one ear stands up, then the other. Then he barks like there's a burglar inside your house. You get up to look, and there's no one there. Then, 10 long seconds later, someone walks past your house with another dog.

That's the sixth sense I'm talking about, and here's how it applies to bouncers. There are 600 people in the club. The band is playing at ear bleeding decibels, and there's a line at the door to get in. Kids are dancing and swaying to the beat, while others are racing to the bar the very second the band goes on break. There are a lot of parts moving at the same time, coupled with a lot of noise. But the bouncers always knew that a certain noise they just heard over all the other noises wasn't normal. It was either a fight in the works or one in play. When this happens, the bouncers move quickly toward the problem, walking quickly but not running so they don't create attention or concern. That's what skilled bouncers do.

On one particular night, the problem was on the dance floor. Some guy knocked into another guy and that guy then knocked into his girlfriend, who lost her drink on the floor. See where this is going? Even though the music is screaming loud, the bouncers from afar could still hear the glass break and move quickly to investigate. Now there are four guys throwing punches, and the band is playing "Highway to Hell," which added more fuel to the fire. Within six or seven seconds, Tommy the Marine, Full Nelson Tommy, Too Tall Greg and Dean have each of the offenders in bear locks and are moving them toward the rear exit. The brawlers are shuffling their feet, which are going nowhere except to the exit. Once they realize the club has overwhelming power, they give up their fight and go limp or suffer the consequences of being hurt while being subdued. Once the problem has been neutralized, the bouncers come back into the club, fix their disheveled clothing, and go back to their assigned positions to wait for the next flare up. It's going to happen again, we just don't know when.

ROCK CLUB PERSONEL
The Walls Can't Talk, but People Can

Looking back, who had a better job than the people at Circus-Circus or any other club for that matter? They mixed and poured drinks, they worked the door, they welcomed our guests, and sometimes they tossed them out on their asses.

They lugged cases of beer up and down staircases all night long.

They collected a paycheck, but more importantly, they collected stories—lots of great stories. That's what we're here for.

We were all in our 20s with the exception of a few kids, and a couple of well-aged characters. Like a well-oiled machine, the employees of The Circus and other rock clubs all over America cranked it out five and six nights a week and then came back for more the next day.

I was fortunate enough to reach out to some of these guys and gals and ask them about their experience working at a rock club in that memorable era.

To add flavor to this story, we've asked them to remember those special, significant, hilarious, and embarrassing nights. Roll the tape, please...

HARRY SWEENEY
BARTENDER
CLUB: CIRCUS-CIRCUS
BERGENFIELD, NEW JERSEY

I delivered mail by day, and drinks at night! I was a bartender at Circus-Circus on weekends and a mail carrier during the week.

Which do you think was more fun?

Are you kidding me? I couldn't wait to go to work...at Circus-Circus, that is! I would leave the club at 3 am on a Friday and go to work at the New Milford post office at 7 am the same morning. Then return to bartend at the club that same night and work until 4 am But I'll tell you the truth, I almost quit in the beginning after the first two fights. It was a little scary. I asked myself, what am I, fucking nuts? I'm married with kids! But then you get used to it after a while and say to yourself, when it happens, it happens. Just be ready for it and get out of the way of flying objects as well as people. At times, it was bedlam. I remember being told that if anyone tries to come over the bar and steal the money, just whack them in the head with a bottle. I picked up a bottle a couple of times anticipating just that. Fortunately, it never happened. I know I'm talking tough, but with ten large bouncers around the club, I could do or say just about anything I wanted to.

Do you have one or two memories that stand out from the others?

I remember the first time I heard the band Condor at the club. They were playing a song called "My Sharona," which I never heard before. The next day I heard that same song on the radio and thought it was Condor. I found out several weeks later that it was actually a band called The Knack! I remember after closing time, going to the Orangeburg Pub in New York with a group of bartenders and bouncers from The Circus, because they were open until 4 am. Then there was the iconic Forum Diner on Route 4 in Paramus that we used to hit after a busy night.

With all the craziness of the time and the lifestyle associated with it, I walked away mostly with good memories, including some life lessons. Yea, I got caught up in the drug and drinking scene like so many others, but was fortunate enough to have survived it. I've been sober now for 22 years. But oh…The memories!

BOB DYNAN
BOUNCER/BARTENDER
CLUBS: DODD'S, THE FINAL EXAM, CREATIONS, DUNES TILL DAWN, ORANGE, RANDOLPH, WEST ORANGE, AND LONGPORT, NEW JERSEY

It was a historic time—you don't realize the history! The clubs, the rock scene, live music…It's all gone!

I have a picture of David Johansen sitting with David Bowie in Max's Kansas City, in New York. You could go to The Capital Theater and see Bruce for $6. The music was great, Bruce was the Boss, and we were God! We were kids…maybe 18 and invincible. Everyone came to New Jersey to get the Asbury Park sound. I was in an Atlantic City casino the first day they opened. I didn't even realize it was history in the making. I just happened to be there because I was heading to south Jersey to work at a club and somehow wound up at a casino.

How many years did you work the club scene and which club or clubs were your most memorable?

I bartended and bounced at several great rooms in Jersey including The Final Exam in Randolph Township, Creations in West Orange, and of course my favorite, Dodd's in Orange. Dodd's to me was the iconic leader in Essex County and probably North Jersey. He had a lot of exclusive deals with bands. I worked at several of the Senator's clubs from 1975 when I was just 18, until 1982 when it was time to settle down.

The late former State Senate President, Frank J. "Pat" Dodd not only wielded power in Essex County but also in the many rock clubs that he owned.

In the summers I worked at a place called Dunes Till Dawn in Longport, New Jersey, right outside Atlantic City. The Senator would rent a house for us guys coming down from North Jersey so we could work the summers in his clubs. I'd split a room with someone else for five dollars a week. The Dunes was a huge three-thousand person capacity club, which opened at 11 am and closed at 7 am. Prime time for us was 3 am when bars up north like D'Jais in Belmar, had to close at 1:30 or 2 am. We had the 23 hour liquor license, because we were in Atlantic County. We called it Dunes till death! When we made last call, we opened the shades on the windows."

How was your social life back then? Lots of poontang?

That may be an understatement. It was crazy times with no shortage of wild women. I can't get into it right now (my wife is right here), but you can imagine! The only place that I had a little trouble was at The Dunes because the girls couldn't last until 7 am. Let's just say the 70s and early 80s didn't suck. Rick…this could be a history book!

DANNY DOONER
CHIEF COOK AND BOTTLE WASHER
CLUB: CIRCUS-CIRCUS
BERGENFIELD, NEW JERSEY

It was a party every night. I can't count the girls I met in that place. It was a freakin' blast. I was the youngest one there. I was 18 and held every position except bartender. From beer runner, to waiter, to cook, to DJ, to occasional bouncer; I did it all and couldn't wait to go to work and do it all over the next day. I'm 51 now, but back then I was the youngest person working in that place. We always had money in our pockets. Money went a long way back then."

Who was your favorite band or bands?

The coolest band to ever play at the club had to have been Wendy O. Williams and the Plasmatics. I saw them on TV right before they played The Circus doing a promotional stunt in New York where they blew up a car on stage or something like that.

What about the drug scene back then?

Hey, I worked in a rock club; it was the 70s and 80s. Having a bag of coke on you was almost like having a pack of cigarettes. Everybody had a bag of coke…everybody! I remember catching two guys doing some lines in one of the back booths, so I confiscated it. You know where that coke went?

The subject of drugs suddenly became somber when I brought up the infamous drug raid that took place at The Circus on December 15, 1982. Dan remembers that night all too well.

I remember the night the cops came to get us. They were in big numbers. I'll never forget this. I'm sitting in the DJ booth and notice three guys on "Joe," whisking him away, and then they grab another bartender and take him out in handcuffs. I knew what this was about. The three of us had just sold an ounce of coke to an undercover agent. A former Glen Rock high school buddy set us up to offset charges that he was facing for distribution and other criminal activity. A plain-clothed agent approached me, and before he even spoke a word, I nervously asked, 'Are you looking for Dan Dooner?' Yes, and he said, "you're under arrest!"

Outside of this blip in the radar and a six-month stint in the county jail, I got my life back on track and continue to work my ass off. People are still talking about that place and time in history.

DONNA RHEAUME
BARTENDER
CLUB: THE SHOWPLACE
DOVER, NEW JERSEY

This old guy pulls into the parking lot in a beat-up station wagon and then gets out of the car with a guitar in his hand. He was all alone. I looked a little closer and it was Chuck Berry.

Although he looked like he had "no particular place to go," Berry was booked to perform at The Showplace that night, and Donna would be one of the bartenders. That old guy she speaks of was about the same age as is Donna today.

I just turned 18 back then, so it was a little intimidating work-ing as a bartender, particularly in a male-dominated business. As a female it wasn't uncommon to be hit on by band members, their road-ies, customers, and others. But overall, it was a great time in my life, and as a kid, I got to see so many great bands and musicians. I met or saw Alvin Bishop, Rick Derringer, Edgar Winter, Iggy Pop, and countless others. Where could you work and get paid to hear that kind of music?

I was flattered when the drummer for Blackfoot told me that I made the best Brandy Alexanders—and by the pitcher no less. I'm sure I wasn't the only bartender he said that to, but it still felt good at the time. And, then there was David Johansen. He sat down at the bar, and we talked like two old-time friends, although we never met before. He was one of the nicest, down- to-earth people you'd ever want to meet. Would he remember me today? Who knows? There were so many.

Donna went on to tell me about other legendary artists that were either on their way up or on their way down that performed at the popular night spot. She recalled the first time she heard The Ramones.

When my friends told me they would be performing at the club I worked in, I said, 'Who the hell are The Ramones?' But I quickly got my first lesson in punk rock when a capacity crowd showed up in their black leather jackets, ripped jeans, and spiked collars. I didn't even know that punk rock existed. I thought it was some kind of sub-culture.

But I do remember the night they played. I said, 'Holy shit! Am I ever going to hear again?' And then, 15 or 20 minutes into their first set, the power box blew out, the place went dark. More than 500 punk rockers in the place were yelling, 'Refund! Refund! Refund!' It was pandemonium. People were reaching over the bar, and that's when my boss told me to lock the cash registers, grab the tip jar, and get out from behind the bar. The fire department and police were there, and the night ended early for everyone, including The Ramones. I recall that they played another night to make up for the disappointment to their fans.

And then there was her encounter with Wendy O. Williams and the Plasmatics.

This cute, petite, and innocent looking strawberry blond was sitting at my bar having a soda. The next thing I know, she's on stage wearing these black leotards and nothing else except for black tape covering her nipples. The guitarist next to her and sporting a bright blue mohawk hairdo, was spitting into the crowd while some of them reciprocated. I found out later that this was tradition with some hard core punk bands, and their followers.

You might say I got a crash course on rock and roll not just from working in a club, but going to other clubs and experiencing the whole scene. It was a different time.

DOUGLAS "JAWS" CARTER
BEER RUNNER
CLUB: CIRCUS-CIRCUS
BERGENFIELD, NEW JERSEY

Back then it was a great place where people gathered, listened to great music, and had a great time! Once you were there, you stayed all night. You didn't leave. You didn't go bar hopping because you came to see a certain band. You drank, and back then, we actually drove home.

I've got a long history with the Bandazian-run businesses.

From the ripe age of 13 and into his college years, Doug worked at every luncheonette, diner, and nightclub the family owned.

I was one of the 'beer runners' at Circus-Circus. It wasn't easy, and sometimes I had to run over people to get the beer to the bars. Hey, I'm 5 feet, 8 inches with platform shoes. Speaking of shoes; with people spilling drinks, broken beer bottles, and walking behind the bars a hundred times a night, your shoes always got ruined. They stuck to the floor. I remember there was a guy that used to stop by the club once a month and sell us shoes out of his trunk for eight dollars. I don't care what shoes you had, they didn't last.

The walk-in beer cooler couldn't have been further from the bars. I'd walk maybe 100 or 200 feet, 40 or 50 times a night. I'd walk up a huge flight of stairs, through the kitchen, and into mass crowds with three cases in my arms. They got heavier and heavier as the night went on. I remember the night Twisted Sister was playing and the fire marshal came in. We were way over capacity and certain we were going to get shut down, but that never happened. I was in charge of collecting the money that night and remember the two 'pillars' standing next to me. These bouncers had to be 6 feet 10 inches. We were told that no one gets in free, and they backed it up.

And your most memorable experience or experiences?

Where do I start? Johnny Thunders was so fucked up he fell over the drum set. Friends was great. I remember the two brothers with the big hair rocking back and forth on stage. They did great "Bruce" and always had the house rocking. Timberwolf on Tuesday nights. The crowd never tipped! Jorma Kaukonen. I never knew he had a full tattoo on his back until a fan showed his and Jorma reciprocated. Wendy O. Williams from The Plasmatics was in the dressing room. I was in charge of making sure that no one got near her. I was kind of the last line of defense in case someone breached security and got through the kitchen and into the dressing room. She had pasties on and although it wasn't my job, I was watching them.

If you had a reunion with everyone that partied in the late 70s and 80s, you'd need Giants Stadium!

Doug, what about the drug scene?

Hey, it was the eighties!

EUGENE INTRONA
SECURITY/BARTENDER/D.J./MANAGER
CLUB: THE SOAP FACTORY
PALISADES PARK, NEW JERSEY
INTERVIEW BY DAN LORENZO

Getting a fake driver's license was a rite of passage for me and my friends. My buddy and I were 17 in 1980. After we purchased our fake IDs in NYC, the first place we attempted to get into was The Soap Factory in Palisades Park, NJ. The Soap Factory was legendary, filled to the rim with beautiful women on a consistent basis. Eugene Introna started out at The Soap Factory working security in 1975. I spoke with him in February 2014.

"I use the word 'security,' I don't use the word 'bouncer' because in the industry that I'm still in today, I think that the word bouncer gives off the wrong connotation. I despise the word bouncer. It makes people who do that job sound like a bunch of fucking idiots. You're looked at as a big, dumb, stupid person whose main intention is to hurt people."

He continued, "In '76-'77 we started transitioning from a disco to a rock venue. The rock scene was starting to perk up. What happened was they started doing a rock night. The first band was E. Walker. Back then we were open from 9 pm until 3 am. Unlike today, people came out at 9 pm. You were packed all night.

"The band scene was already pretty alive at Mother's and Topaz. When we started doing it, it started happening on a bigger scale. I was on my way to becoming a manager, and I said to the manager, Jimmy, 'This is really weird. What's going on here? We had 1,600 people in the club and the DJ booth had a lock on the door so nobody could get in. The same record played over-and-over during the band's break!' I said, 'We can't do that!'

The next week, I brought some records from home. I had about eight albums. It was easy for me to multitask, so during the band's break I played the music. Six months later I owned 10,000 albums. I had every record promotion company in my face. I had every A+R guy in my face. I started learning about the record business. As we expanded eventually, The Soap Factory became a full-time rock venue. One of the most-watched bands by talent scouts was T. Roth and Another Pretty Face. Everybody was mesmerized by that guy."

I can vouch for Eugene as my band, Hades, once opened up for Twisted Sister at The Soap Factory. It was virtually impossible to get to the stage; it was so crowded. Eugene told me the legal capacity was about 1,600 to 1,700 occupants. A band such as White Tiger could bring that many people...on a Wednesday night.

Eugene said, "We had vertical nights with Condor and Friends and Zebra."

Rick Bandazian asked me to question Eugene about which bands came in with an attitude. Mr. Introna surprised me with his answer.

"None of them. I was friendly with them. They knew that I did the radio and the marketing. The guys from Twisted Sister were cool as hell. David Johansen came in after leaving the New York Dolls. He was cool. When I booked Aerosmith after Joe Perry left the band. I remember Steven Tyler walking in for sound check. The first thing he asked was, 'Where's the coke?' I was like, 'Oh boy.' It really wasn't about that. The guys of Twisted Sister were complete businessmen. They were straight as hell. When they took their make-up off they were just regular guys. The same thing with Zebra. The same thing with Jesse Bolt. They were an incredible band. They were showcasing at Great Gildersleeves twice a month on a Monday night.

"The Soap Factory was "the" room. The only reason The Stone Pony had its reputation was because Springsteen and Southside Johnny lived down there."

The large building that was once The Soap Factory still sits at 15 Grand Avenue. An influx of Koreans to the area is why you may not be able to read some of the signs in the surrounding neighborhood. The patrons who visit the poorly named Mariachi Club have no idea what a legendary room they are in.

CHRIS MADDEN
BARTENDER
CLUB: CIRCUS-CIRCUS
BERGENFIELD, NEW JERSEY

Drink ordering was done in sign language when the band was playing, because you couldn't hear anything other than the band. I should've written a handbook on this special way of communicating for drinks. I'll never forget working the band room bar, especially when the band was known to play at eardrum-splitting decibels. We had to actually remove the glassware from the shelves, or they would vibrate off and onto the floor.

The staff at the club was like family. Everyone watched each other's back. We had our share of fights, particularly on nickel beer night, when it got pretty crazy. But the bouncers stayed on top of things. There was beer all over the place, including the floor, the bar, and on the patrons. On occasion, when things seemed to get out of control, the bartenders would hop over the bar and lend a hand.

Did you have any experience behind the bar before Circus-Circus?

I worked at two places before Circus-Circus. One was a rough bar in Bloomfield and the other was a fine dining restaurant in Paterson. I didn't know much about Circus-Circus beforehand, but soon found it would be like attending the Mad Hatter's Tea Party of the 20th century. I didn't know what I was in for," he revealed. "It was a much younger crowd than I was used to. Here I was 35 years old and everyone around me, 18 or 20.

The club always seemed to attract a high level of talent with big names such as Steppenwolf, Twisted Sister, Mountain, The Good Rats, and the best local bands the area had to offer.

That had to be the craziest and most exciting place I've ever worked in my life.

ANDREW POLITI
MANAGER, BARTENTER, BOUNCER
CLUBS: OSPREY HOTEL, MANASQUAN, NJ
THE ROYAL MANOR NORTH, NORTH BRUNSWICK, NJ
THE FACTORY, STATEN ISLAND, NY

It's like they paid me to go out at night and have a good time. It was great working in the club scene. I had a great run from 1978 to 1983. If I could relive five years of my life, it would be those five.

Andrew looked older for his age, so it was never a problem getting into most clubs at just 17 years old. Most of the time, they never even proofed him.

My friends and I would look at The Aquarian Weekly and decide what club we were going to that night and which band or bands we were going to see. There were so many choices back then, but one of my favorite bands to see live was Salty Dog, which performed regularly at The Osprey in Manasquan. After being a regular patron myself at many of the clubs and enjoying the scene, I thought it would be cool if I could get a job at one. My life was getting a little boring as a lifeguard, so I was looking for a change.

As luck would have it, a friend of mine was a bouncer at The Osprey and introduced me to the manager. I was hired on the spot, and just like all new employees, I started on the floor as a bouncer. If you wanted to be a bartender or move up in the club, that's where you started. For a while I bounced, bartended, and then managed.

If you went to a club during that era, more specifically a rock club, the odds were much greater that you would see a male bartender than a female. The logic was simple. When the fights break out, or worse a brawl, you would have additional muscle that would jump over the bar to assist the bouncers. Usually!

Besides The Osprey, Andrew also worked at two other popular night spots; The Royal Manor North in North Brunswick and The Factory in Staten Island.

It was great to work the different rooms. Every club had its unique clientele. As an employee, it was phenomenal to have worked at all of them. I got to see, or at least hear, some of the greatest bands and musicians that anyone could imagine. The high quality of music that came from the Tri-State area was just amazing. Bruce, Southside Johnny, Beaver Brown, Twisted Sister, Bon Jovi, The Ramones, and too many others to remember, all went on to commercial success. And, look at the guys from Phantom's Opera that joined Bon Jovi? I give these guys all the credit in the world.

The cover bands were no slouches either. Some of the guys and gals in these bands just wanted to be successful club musicians, like Lenny Molinari from Yasgur's Farm. He's got to be one of the top guitarists to come out of the area.

Summarize the late 70s and early 80s in a sentence or two.

It was the best of times to go out, party, and meet people. And of course, we didn't have the Internet so if you wanted to hook-up you went to a club. And hook-up, we did!

Tonight:
New Riders of the Purple Sage, Featuring the ABC
January 29, 1981

The New Riders of the Purple Sage were like a lot of 70s bands in the early mid-70s. With a hippie-retro cowboy look, a mix of country and rock and folk, and some marijuana references to seal their hippie credentials, they all blended together with tight harmonies and a studio's polish.

The New Riders, as they're often called, signed to Columbia Records in 1971 by legendary record exec Clive Davis. They created their first album, *New Riders of the Purple Sage*, and it was an instant radio and commercial hit. If you were pretty hip in the early 70s, this was stuff you thought was equally hip.

The band owed its inception to the Grateful Dead in one of its many extracurricular inceptions. In fact, Robert Hunter and Mickey Hart, both original members of the Dead, were also original members of the band. The band was part Gram Parsons, part Burrito Brothers, part Poco, part all that early, original country-rock, just before The Eagles came along.

It would only be a couple of years later that they had their first gold record, "The Adventures of Panama Red." ('Yer basic hippie dude character.) They played at huge venues such as Kezar Stadium in San Francisco and RFK Stadium in Washington, DC, opening for the Dead and others. So, we're talking pretty major league rock stars here!

So, here we are once again. It's Friday night. The club isn't packed yet, but it's getting busy. Maybe a 300 count so far, and my father is working the door with two bouncers checking IDs and collecting tickets. Who knew, really, who the band was going to attract that evening?

It isn't long before my father sent one of the bouncers to tell me the ABC (Alcoholic Beverage Control) is at the entrance. I walked over and asked if there was a problem. The two agents, a male and female, told me they just wanted to look around. I said, "No problem," although it wasn't like I had a choice.

Now I'm a little paranoid and praying that everyone in the club is of age, and we're not doing anything illegal. I'm trying to shadow the ABC agents inconspicuously but as the crowd is beginning to grow, they become harder to follow. What if someone in the club lights up a joint, and the ABC agents smell it? What if they walk into the bathroom and someone's doing a line?

I walk behind the main bar (one of three), which was about 50 feet long and ran the length of the wall. I'm doing a peripheral scan of the place from behind the bar, and I notice that the agents are talking to someone in one of the booths. As I'm watching, one of the agents turns to me and we lock eyes on each other. He motions me to come over. He then proceeds to tell me that the girl in the booth with a drink in front of her is under age. I looked into the dimly light booth and found myself staring down at this petite blond wearing a black tight sweater and a gold chain with a silver cross hanging over the front of her full-busted chest. She could have been a nun. I asked the girl to show me her ID and she pulls out her license. After asking her to stand, I eyeballed the license carefully, which matched her height, weight, and eye color almost perfectly. I called over the bouncer proofing people at the door and asked if he remembered her coming in.

My bouncer, Dean, who never forgets a face, said he did and that she not only had one form of proof, but showed him three. It may have been a college ID and credit card. I can't remember which IDs she had, but remember—back then it was easy to get fake ID.

The agents brought her into our office and asked that she call her parents. Whether trying to be cute, or just frightened, the girl called someone else and tried to pretend that it was her mother. After the agents threatened her with arrest, she eventually called her house and her mother got on the phone with the agent. The mother confirmed that her IDs were fake, and she was underage.

After the girl identified the bartender who served her, the agents wanted him arrested, so they called the Bergenfield Police Department. A young detective showed up a short time later and began talking to the agents. I tried to listen in over the blaring music but couldn't hear very much. I instinctively knew it wasn't good. The detective was a really cool guy who we got to know pretty well since we opened the club two years before. He was one of the few law enforcement officials that liked our club and always supported us when there was a problem. He was probably in his late 20s, early 30s, and would stop in our place from time to time—while on duty no less—for a couple of drinks. I'm not telling tales out of school, that's just the way it was back then.

Anyway, the two ABC agents and the detective told me that they had to bring the bartender to police headquarters to book him for serving a minor. Of course, I expressed my opinion of how ridiculous that was, but it didn't matter. At that point, the bartender knew the scoop and came from around the bar to cooperate. One of the agents said to the detective, "Aren't you going to handcuff him?" The detective said, "No, I won't. I know these people."

We went to court, pleaded no contest, and were given a choice. Pay a $2,500 fine or close for 30 days. We obviously paid the fine but did so in protest.

After the court appearance, I met the ABC agent in the hallway and asked him how, exactly, were we to know when someone is underage, when they show good ID and in this case, three good IDs.

His brilliant response: "Don't let people into your club who look young."

I really wanted to say, "Seriously, Genius? Fuck you."

Oh yeah…and The New Riders of the Purple Sage played that night.

Road Warriors

Now the seats are all empty
Let the roadies take the stage
Pack it up and tear it down
They're the first to come and last to leave
Working for that minimum wage
They'll set it up in another town…

—"The Load-Out" by Jackson Browne

No one worked harder than the roadies, although Mr. Browne notwithstanding, they didn't do it for minimum wage. Still, the roadies were the ones "without whom…"

The roadies make the show happen—the sound, the lights, the plugs, and the power associated with every gig. Without them, there is no show. They were the guys who had to fix a frazzled cable, holding it in place, while trying to locate that last roll of duct tape that fell out of the cart and into the snow. In the dark. Ten minutes before show time.

And every variation of that scenario. Constantly.

Load it. Unload it. Set it up. Power it. Repair it. Take it all down. Load it up again. And again.

Roadies sleep late. They eat junk food. They love the road. They're not rock stars, and they know it. They might have had those dreams at one time, but by the time you're on a band's payroll, there's no rocking for you. Only rolling. Rolling in. Rolling out. Rolling up. So, they sleep until noon.

The band's equipment trucks get unloaded around four in the afternoon for a show that starts at 9:30 or 10 pm. Sound equipment and lights, they usually run both. Most local bands couldn't afford to pay for both.

They work through two or three sets with the band, constantly watching each and every move to make sure the show is going smoothly—the lights go on and off as planned, and nothing breaks.

When a cymbal stand falls? Rush over and right it. An amp blows? Have another one ready. A string breaks? Get a guitar in the guitarist's hands stat, while you replace the broken string before the next song is done. A good roadie's concentration is completely focused during the show; he's easily working as hard as the band—and with speed and grace to boot.

If you're a big band touring nationally or internationally, you don't just have roadies; you have a tour manager. He or she has a laundry list of things to do. This is the guy or gal who keeps everyone on schedule, deals with buses or limos, gets the group to the show on time, arranges meals, and fields any and all of the problems associated with the tour. The tour manager is also the point person for radio, TV, magazine, or other media interviews. The tour manager also has to be smart in selecting the right roadies to get the job done, night after night, efficiently, and on schedule.

It goes without saying that a roadie needs to be perfectly cool under pressure, no matter the circumstance. It is one thing to rush center stage to fix a dead mike, but quite another to escape a possible club fire.

Our ceiling almost went up once from pyrotechnics ignited by some band's idiot managers or tour managers.

It was supposed to look like a fireworks display on the right and left sides of the stage. When the flash pods went off, they hit the ceiling like a blowtorch, and the ceiling started smoldering. It took two full fire extinguishers to put it out. I was in a panic the whole time, not knowing if the fire was hidden in the ceiling.

Recall that in 2003, the band Great White was playing at The Station nightclub in Rhode Island. A fire broke out from pyrotechnics lit indoors. One hundred people died and more than 200 were injured. Ultimately, tour manager Daniel Michel Biechele, 29, from Orlando, Florida, pled guilty to 100 counts of involuntary manslaughter and was sentenced to 15 years in state prison. He served just less than four years, with 11 years suspended.

The club's owners, Michael and Jeffrey Derderian, were scheduled to go on trial for 100 counts of manslaughter, following Biechele's trial. They changed their pleas, however, on September 21, 2006, before Superior Court Judge Francis J. Darigan, from not guilty to no contest. They wanted to avoid a trial.

Michael Derderian received 15 years in prison, with four served and 11 years suspended, plus three years' probation—the same sentence as Biechele. Jeffrey Derderian received a 10-year suspended sentence, three years' probation, and 500 hours of community service. The Derderians were also fined $1.07 million for failing to carry workers' compensation insurance for their employees, four of whom died in the blaze. As of August 2008, various defendants in settlement proceedings have offered nearly $175 million to the families of the victims.

But now, the show's over and it's two or three in the morning and everyone's exhausted, and a little drunk.

The second shift now commences. The roadies break everything down, put the equipment back in the trucks, and get home at maybe five or six am. Then, they sleep, sleep, sleep.

It always seemed to me that roadies had an unfair reputation for being lugs, because they were the workhorses who did the heavy lifting day in and day out, week after week.

But a real roadie is smart and resourceful. And practical. Very few of them harbor dreams of stardom anymore. They love seeing a show run smoothly and being part of a team. They're usually more gearhead than Deadhead, too, so they love tinkering with equipment—a valuable trait for a roadie to have.

And, a trustworthy and professional roadie is worth his weight in gold. As the key guys for any successful show, they have to be both electrician and ambassador. They have to deal with club owners and the people with whom they come in contact before, during, and after the gig.

And certainly there are club owners who are tougher than others to deal with. Objectively speaking, I honestly think bands would prefer to play The Circus more than other clubs, because, frankly, I learned early on that being a decent person goes a pretty long way in making friends and keeping customers (and bands) happy.

So, here's to all roadies, tour managers, stage managers, caterers, drivers, and all levels of rock and rolldom who work tirelessly to locate .005 Dunlop guitar picks in the middle of the night, patch up jeans, mop up spills, deal with club owners, and make sure those guitars don't bounce around in the back of the truck.

You're the first to come and the last to leave. It never goes unappreciated.

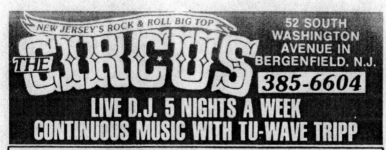

NEW JERSEY'S ROCK & ROLL BIG TOP
THE CIRCUS

52 SOUTH WASHINGTON AVENUE IN BERGENFIELD, N.J.

385-6604

LIVE D.J. 5 NIGHTS A WEEK
CONTINUOUS MUSIC WITH TU-WAVE TRIPP

EVERY MONDAY IN AUGUST

LADIES DRINK FREE
FROM 8:30 PM TIL 10:00 PM
Complements of The Moderns

TUESDAY AUGUST 3

BLACK SABBITH
OZZY OSBOURNE SHOW
LADIES DRINK FREE
FROM 8:30 PM TIL 10:00 PM
Complements of EQUINOX

TUESDAY AUGUST 10, 17, 24, 31

ALL MALE BURLESQUE

PLUS FEMALE IMPERSONATOR
SHOW STARTS AT 8:30 PM
CALL FOR TABLE RESERVATIONS
GUYS WELCOME AFTER MIDNIGHT

WEDNESDAY AUGUST 4	WEDNESDAY AUGUST 11, 18, 25
ACOUSTIC **Jorma Kaukonen** WITH SPECIAL GUEST **TIMBERWOLF**	**TIMBERWOLF** TRIBUTE TO THE GRATEFUL DEAD

EVERY THURSDAY IN AUGUST

COVER CHARGE
INCLUDES ALL
YOU CAN DRINK
FROM 8:30-10:30 P.M.

BIKINI CONTEST
Free Admission To Contestants
Free Tank Top To Participants
$100 ....First Prize
$50 ....Second Prize
$25 ....Third Prize

FRI AUG 6	FRI AUG 13	FRI AUG 20	FRI AUG 27
TIMBERWOLF TRIBUTE TO THE GRATEFUL DEAD	Condor ROCKS THE 80'S	WHITE TIGER	MOLLY CRIBB

NOW OPEN MON-FRI FOR THE SUMMER

David Johansen and Johnny Thunders:
Two Stars, One Personality Crisis

His band came crashing onto the scene somewhere in the mid-70s, upending a world of mellow soft rock, disco, Stevie Wonder, and a buffet table full of earnest singer–songwriters. They were evoking the new rock and roll glam movement—T-Rex, Lou Reed, David Bowie, the Stones, Aerosmith, and Mott the Hoople, with just a *soupçon* of the Shangri-Las.

They were the New York Dolls. They were led by singer–songwriter–personality David Johansen, a pouty-lipped amalgam of style and attitude, along with his running buddy, the sloppy chic, droopy-eyed Johnny Thunders.

To be honest, they weren't for everyone. But if you got it, you really got it. To this day, those who were influenced by this band or those that actually saw the raucous band in its heyday, never forgot them.

By the time Mr. Johansen made his debut at The Circus, The Dolls were far behind him. He had moved on. He had become a solo artist, one of many styles and colors—still a rocker, but one who could see that there was a huge palette of musical styles from which he could draw inspiration. He would soon create his cartoon-ish Louie Prima–Ricky Ricardo persona, "Buster Poindexter," as his next incarnation, miles away in style and substance from The Dolls.

I can't forget the afternoon David Johansen showed up for the regular sound check. It didn't seem like the regular concert I was accustomed to, but rather a Broadway production, with an outrageous light and sound show; it was more theater than rock.

Come show time, the energetic crowd pushed and shoved its way to get closer to the stage, although the barricades made it difficult to get too close.

Johansen saluted his influences, his history, and glimpses of his future all at once. With "It's My Life," "Personality Crisis," and "We've Gotta Get Out of this Place," it was all there, but David wasn't the pansexual wonder he was with The Dolls. He had grown up.

You could tell from looking at the crowd that Johansen had a loyal fan base; the Morrissey of his time. And, he took full advantage.

Then there was his associate, Johnny Thunders, who also played The Circus, but under slightly different circumstances. His show almost didn't come off at all.

It was 10:30 pm and the opening act had just finished their set. The plan was for Thunders to go on at midnight. But there was no sign of the headliner.

Their road manager was pacing the floor, looking panicked. My brother took him aside and learned that Johnny was at some bar on the lower east side of New York City and needed a ride to the club! We grabbed two bouncers off the floor and off they went into the city on their rock and roll rescue mission.

Now I was starting to wonder whether they would even get him back in time to perform. And what shape would he be in?

While the DJ was spinning punk tunes to try and keep the crowd happy, I was drinking one vodka Collins after the next, smoking like a chimney, and looking at my watch every five minutes. My brother was doing pretty much the same, while my father was bitching at him for booking the band in the first place. I used to joke that, "When my brother booked the money makers, my father never remembered, but when he booked the losers, he never forgot!"

The crowd was getting restless and beginning to inquire about when the band would come on, unaware that the headliner wasn't even in the house. After all, it was now 12:30 am. Without cell phones in those days, we were in the dark.

A short time later, I noticed a commotion at the door and saw Johnny Thunders stumbling into the club, propped up by the guys we sent to get him.

Within minutes, the bouncers literally lifted him by his arms and strategically placed him on the stage by the microphone. The band started playing, and Thunders suddenly lit up like a Christmas toy with new batteries.

The mostly punk crowd loved him. He came out of the gate with his most memorable tune, the plaintive, "You Can't Put Your Arms Around a Memory," a song that took its title from a line in the '50s Jackie Gleason sitcom, *The Honeymooners*. He only did one set because of his tardiness, but by that time it was late, and most of the crowd was ready to head for home.

No one in the crowd knew that an hour before, Thunders was lying on a street corner in New York City, wasted, most likely on heroin (his current addiction).

Johnny Thunders went on to form his own band, The Heartbreakers (no relation to Tom Petty's band), and although he never sounded like The Sex Pistols or The Ramones, he was a true pioneer in punk rock, long before mainstream rock fans knew what "punk" was.

Heroin, his drug of choice, took him off life's stage at only 42. But it was the fastest and loudest 42 years ever.

Joe Perry Draws the Line

Aerosmith is a band in the true rock and roll tradition—hard rocking and hard fighting. Lead singer Steven Tyler admitted on more than one occasion—and to more than one source, most recently *60 Minutes*—to snorting five to six million dollars of cocaine into his nose. And, his fights with lead guitarist Joe Perry were legendary.

Once, in a memorable, heated backstage skirmish in Cleveland in 1979, an enraged Perry actually threw a glass of milk at band member Tom Hamilton's wife. Following that tussle, yet another argument with Tyler resulted in Perry leaving the band for five years. During that time, he actually considered joining both Metallica and Alice Cooper's band.

During his time away from Aerosmith with no reunion on the horizon, he formed the Joe Perry Project with singer Mach Bell, bassist Danny Hargrove, and drummer Joe Pet. He signed a contract with Aerosmith's own label, Columbia.

The band's debut album, "Let the Music Do the Talking" was a strong musical effort and even garnered a hit track of the same name; but, as radio and fans let him know, it wasn't Aerosmith. But live, none of that mattered. On April 3, 1982, fans could see Joe Perry up close at The Circus and hear his hard-driving style of rock right in front of their faces.

After his sound check, I had the chance to say hello to Joe and have a drink with him. Back then, I really didn't think it was a big deal talking to any of these performers, because, frankly, I had no idea who anyone was.

My brother was the guy booking the acts and the one who knew what act would pack the place (most times, anyway). I didn't even bother getting autographs from most of these performers, because it didn't seem like that big a deal at the time. One of the few autographs I did get, interestingly enough, was Joe's. It now hangs proudly in my family room with other Circus-Circus memorabilia.

One of my very dear friends, Dirk Vuijst, used to come to The Circus often to check out bands, particularly recording artists. Back then, when I casually mentioned to Dirk that The Joe Perry Project would be playing at our club, he was over the moon. I brought Dirk backstage to meet Joe and get the requested number of autographs. To this day, he still reminds me of that evening. At age 60, Dirk is still rocking it and playing bass for a local New Jersey rock band called The Knight Crawlers.

Like every other band that played our club, security led Joe Perry and his band through the crowd to the stage. There was no direct route to the stage without going right through the crowd, and on this night, the place was once again packed.

Moving slowly across the floor surrounded by a security cordon, Joe jumped onto the stage with his band, strummed a chord or two, nodded at the drummer, and off they went —flat-out, hard-charging metal rock.

It wasn't Aerosmith, but it didn't need to be.

The Joe Perry Project returned to The Circus for another concert on October 22, 1982. It was great, but he was competing against himself. Let's call it a draw.

		Thurs Apr 1	Fri Apr 2	Sat Apr 3
NOW OPEN TUESDAYS		TIMBERWOLF TRIBUTE TO THE GREATFUL DEAD *Happy Hour Til 11 PM*	Back Streets TRIBUTE TO THE BOSS	JOE PERRY PROJECT *Tickets At Door Only*
Tues Apr 6	Wed Apr 7	Thurs Apr 8	Fri Apr 9	Sat Apr 10 *In Concert*
STICKY FINGERS TRIBUTE TO THE ROLLING STONES	BLUE EMERALD *Free Drink With Admission*	TIMBERWOLF TRIBUTE TO THE GREATFUL DEAD *Happy Hour Til 11 PM*	Nursery Cryme	Crystal Ship RENAISSANCE OF THE DOORS
Tues Apr 13	Wed Apr 14	Thurs Apr 15	Fri Apr 16	Sat Apr 17
STICKY FINGERS TRIBUTE TO THE ROLLING STONES	BLUE EMERALD *Free Drink With Admission*	TIMBERWOLF TRIBUTE TO THE GREATFUL DEAD *Happy Hour Til 11 PM*	The Rose *The Janis Joplin Show*	MOLLY GRIBB
Tues Apr 20	Wed Apr 21	Thurs Apr 22	Fri Apr 23	Sat Apr 24
STICKY FINGERS TRIBUTE TO THE ROLLING STONES	BLUE EMERALD *Free Drink With Admission*	TIMBERWOLF TRIBUTE TO THE GREATFUL DEAD *Happy Hour Til 11 PM*	Call Club For Info	THE WHO SHOW
Tues Apr 27	Wed Apr 28	Thurs Apr 29	Fri Apr 30	Sat May 1
STICKY FINGERS TRIBUTE TO THE ROLLING STONES	BLUE EMERALD *Free Drink With Admission*	TIMBERWOLF TRIBUTE TO THE GREATFUL DEAD *Happy Hour Til 11 PM*	PAPA JOHN CREACH *In Concert*	

THE CIRCUS — NEW JERSEY'S ROCK & ROLL BIG TOP

52 SOUTH WASHINGTON AVENUE IN BERGENFIELD, N.J.

385-6604

APRIL CONCERT SERIES

NON-STOP DANCING 5 NIGHTS A WEEK WITH D.J. TRIPP & OUR SUPER SOUND SYSTEM

JOE PERRY

Collins/Barrasso
280 Lincoln Street
Allston/Boston, MA 02134
617 783 1100

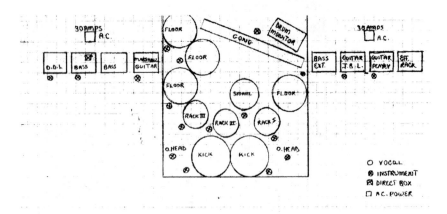

○ VOCAL
⊗ INSTRUMENT
⊠ DIRECT BOX
☐ A.C. POWER

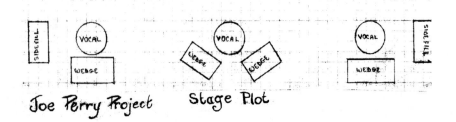

Joe Perry Project   Stage Plot

Tonight's Menu Special: Humble Pie

If you were a rock fan in the mid-70s, you knew the band Humble Pie. Originally formed in 1971, they were led by the diminutive, gravel-voiced soul shouter Steve Marriott. Steve had enjoyed some success as a member of the Small Faces before being replaced by Rod Stewart. On guitar was Peter Frampton, who would go on to create one of the most successful live rock and roll albums in the History of Civilization in 1975's "Frampton Comes Alive." The band enjoyed a slew of US and English hits and toured constantly.

In 1982, long after much of the steam had left the band, Marriott was living in Atlanta. He was back on the road across America with Jim Leverton (bass, backing vocals), former Steppenwolf keyboardist Goldy McJohn, and Chicago-born drummer Fallon Williams III. The original idea was that the band would be billed as The Official Receivers, or maybe The Three Trojans (after McJohn allegedly was let go for his drug habit), or even The Pie. But they naturally ended up being billed by greedy promoters as Humble Pie.

The remaining trio toured Australia in October 1982, billed mostly as the Small Faces to entice unknowing patrons. It was one of the last formal lineups of the band until at least 1989; by that time Steve Marriott was no longer involved.

You get one guess as to where Humble Pie didn't play that year.

It was May1ˢᵗ, 1982. That's one day I'll never forget. Yet another snake-hearted promoter had sold us a Humble Pie show, although it's likely that the band never even knew about the gig.

No matter. The band was a no-show and we were left "30 days in the hole." (Okay, sorry!)

Here's how the promotion thing went. Each month, an index card-sized calendar was given to customers at the door detailing our upcoming shows. Thousands of refrigerators in dorms and apartments throughout the Tri-State area had these cards securely attached with brightly colored magnets, often in the shapes of fruits.

But, I digress.

Sometime in mid-April of 1982, we began to hand out the schedule for May, which we thought had a pretty strong lineup.

There was the aforementioned Humble Pie, Commander Cody ("My Pappy said, 'Son, you're gonna drive me to drinkin' if you don't stop driving that Hot. Rod. Lincoln."), and Robert Hunter (lyricist for The Grateful Dead) in the mix, along with some great cover and tribute bands.

Our show calendar was usually promoted on radio and in local newspapers, especially when we had national acts. In many cases, the bands and their management teams would contractually require it. And, contracts for entertainment were signed weeks and sometimes months in advance. With the exception of the Humble Pie contract.

It never came. Jack called the promoter several times and each time was told, "It's in the mail!" I believe he was also told that wolverines made good house pets!

Jack usually checked out promoters, especially a new one who had no track record with us. But John Scher, co-founder of The Capital Theatre in Passaic, New Jersey and one of the biggest promoters in the business, knew this guy and told us he never had a problem with him. I'm sure that was the case.

So the radio commercials aired: *"Hurry, hurry, hurry to The Circus! This Saturday night May 1ˢᵗ live on stage, Humble Pie!"* with their hit "30 Days in the Hole" rocking in the background. And, it continued, *"Tickets will be sold at the door for this event"* as "I Don't Need no Doctor" spun underneath. *"Doors open at 8:30 pm!"*

That radio spot played all week on two of New York's hottest rock stations, to the tune of $3,000. As required, we leased a professional sound and lighting package. Then there was the print advertising, plus a $750 deposit (about $2,150 in today's dollars), which we never saw again, and an entire staff of employees that was sent home. All totaled, we lost about $5,000 ($14,338 in today's dollars) for just that one night and earned some serious egg on our faces for not delivering the show. Customers who came out to rock on that rainy Saturday night were disappointed to say the least. Many had traveled great distances to see the show.

I spoke to fans that had driven in from as far away as Connecticut, New York City, upstate New York, Delaware, Pennsylvania, and just about everywhere in between.

I don't blame the band, but rather the promoter who left us high and dry.

Not too long after the Humble Pie episode, we learned that other clubs were advertising appearances for the group, one of which was The Fountain Casino in Aberdeen Township, New Jersey, about an hour's drive south of us. The only thing I remember about the owners is that they were really nice Italian guys. I didn't want them to get fucked the way we did. After all, we didn't see each other as competitors, because we were such a long distance apart. Plus, The Fountain Casino was in a different league than we were with a capacity four times our size.

I called one of the owners and told him the story about our no-show. He said, "It's funny you're calling now. The booking agent is here right now. You wanna talk to him?"

"No, no no," I said. "Keep him there. I'm on my way." I grabbed a couple bouncers and off we went, straight down 95 south.

By the time we arrived, he had vanished.

Now, what have we learn from this, class? Well, if you wanna book a big rock band for your class reunion or corporate event, google the promoter's name along with the words "complaint" or "scam." Then, check to see how many versions of your favorite band are out there touring. There might be a few of them.

Oh, and you might want to check the calendar and some obituary pages.

Then, rock out. You've been warned!

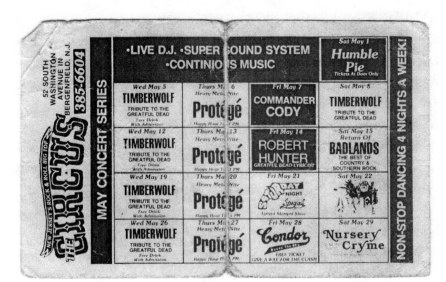

Cover Me: The Life of a Bar Band

"You're cool and cred like Fogerty,
I'm Elvis Presley in the 70s
You're Chateauneuf, I'm Yellow Label
You're the buffet, I'm just the table
I'm a Ford Tempo, you're a Maserati
You're The Great One, I'm Marty McSorley
You're the Concord, I'm economy
I make the dough, but you get the glory."

-Kathleen Edwards, "I Make the Dough, You get the Glory"

This is what it's like when you're one of the hottest cover bands around. You get up early for work, and you work six hours on your shift. You tell the boss it's a show night, and you get the hell out. You head home for a quick nap and a shower.

You drive over to Steve's, or Eric's, or Dan's house, because that's where the truck is, and it's your turn to drive. You help load the truck, according to the checklist. Drums in first, then the PA, then the amps to secure everything else. And, all those cables and cords. Guitars go in the cars.

You have to be where you have to be with no delays or interruptions (you hope), because there are no cell phones to keep each other posted. If you break down, you better hope there's a phone booth nearby.

It's about 4:45 in the afternoon. It's hot and humid. Your teeshirt is drenched. You need a shower again.

Or it's freezing cold. The wind smacks you silly across your face, and you hope you can feel your fingers again later.

You arrive at the load-in. If you're lucky, you have a roadie and a sound guy. The truck doors open, the ramps come out, and the load-in begins. That unique smell of amps, electronics, and metal parts fills the air. You lug equipment in for about 30 minutes. The rest of the band arrives, and you begin to set up your space. Your guitar goes here, this plugs in there; you unravel cables, you flip this switch, that switch, and build your little on-stage universe.

A few hours later, you're doing a quick sound check, making sure that everything works, and that all of the equipment has survived another load-in, gig, and load-out. That's if you're lucky, and there's no headliner. If you're the opener, you have to set up your stuff fast, push it to the back of the stage, and then hurry up and wait.

Some two hours later, "Heart of Glass" by Blondie and then something by Pat Benatar on stage, cranking out your letter perfect version of "Blue Letter" by Fleetwood Mac, follow you.

With a new wave revolution going on, there's Led Zeppelin, there's all that stuff by The Eagles. It didn't matter. You played it all.

The crowd eats it up, screaming for every radio hit they recognize. They're screaming for the songs, not for you.

Sure, the singer is cute, and he sounds just like that guy from Boston, and your drummer shows up with a different girl each gig. But you're a cover band. You play somebody else's hits.

If you're smart, you've got a plan—you've got another set list, one with a lot of originals, and you're waiting for the night that the guy from the record company finally shows up, just like he said he might. You know that Van Halen started out as a cover band. Hell, so did The Beatles.

It could happen.

Until then, you learn the hits, note by note, slowing down the record until you can nail that solo down. Just like the record.

Time Won't Let Me:
Where are Those Talented Musicians Today?

T hey played in bars and clubs night after night, sometimes six and seven nights a week. It was the late 70s, early 80s; a time that can't be measured by what they sang necessarily, but rather what they gave on stage, even when they weren't singing their own songs.

It didn't matter to them, so it seemed, whether there were 40 or 400 people on the dance floor. They played every night with passion, with the intensity and emotion of the original artists.

I'll never forget those guys and gals in so many of the great bands that rocked clubs like ours, all over the region and all over America.

I've reached out to as many musicians as possible through social media, the telephone, sometimes even with pen and paper.

There were so many more talented musicians that rocked our world back in the day… I wish I could have included everyone in this segment; perhaps in another edition or another book!

Set the WayBack Machine for the 70s and '80s, Sherman! Here's what they're remembering and saying about that special time in rock and roll history. Our time!

LENNY MOLINARI
ROCK GROUP "YASGUR'S FARM"

It was the biggest 'cover scene' the world has ever known. There was never one like it before, and there was never another like it since.

August 15, 1969…. Woodstock, billed as "Three days of peace and music" was held in Bethel, New York in the Catskill Mountains on 600 acres owned by dairyman Max B. Yasgur. Four hundred thousand people attended….some say more. Thirty-three musical acts performed at the iconic event, including Janis Joplin, Jefferson Airplane, Leslie West, Jimmy Hendrix, and others.

A decade later, an idea was born, and the music from the Woodstock era would survive with a little help from a rock group called Yasgur's Farm. The concept was simple: bring back to life the music from that special era, and play it with the intensity of the original artists or better. And, if you weren't lucky enough to make it to Woodstock or your parents didn't let you go, Yasgur's Farm would take you there musically.

'*Yasgur's Farm was a labor of love,*' explained lead guitarist and founder of the popular group, Lenny Molinari. *We wanted to keep the flame of that music alive and didn't want it to fade away. We wanted that music to be respected and new generations to be turned on to it. We weren't just playing covers. We had this torch we were carrying and that gave us a feeling of accomplishment in Yasgur's Farm.*

I asked Lenny to recall the first time he ever picked up a guitar, and what noticeable changes had occurred in the club scene over the years. And, of course...where's Yagur's Farm today?

I started when rock and roll started...50 years ago. I began playing at 13 and in clubs, at 15. By the time I was 16, I was making more money than my dad. He used to drive me to clubs. I've done it my whole life. I love music...Thank God I never had to do anything but music my entire life.

What's left today of the club scene are restaurants and more restaurants. There's no place to play. I feel sorry for the bands today. You're either a big touring band, or you're in a garage somewhere. If you're lucky enough to have a gig at all, you've got to wait around for that couple in the corner table to finish desert before you can set up the drum set and all the equipment you just lugged in by yourself. It's all changed now. There's no stage, no sound check...it's disgusting. There are no real nightclubs anymore. Back in the day there were clubs that would even build a loading dock for the bands, and a cold case of cold beer was waiting for you in the dressing room when you arrived. Even if you were a B or C band, you played a lot and could make $500 a *night, even if you didn't have a following. That's the same pay you'd get today, only now, it's 35 years later. If you were an A- band you could play five or six nights a week and make $2,500 a night. It was serious business back then.*

Jackson Browne made me an offer to tour with them, but I turned it down because I was making more playing the circuit at home. It was very professional back then and the money kept rolling in. You could tour the bars in our area and make as much money as a band touring the country and at the end of the night go home and sleep in your own bed.

The bands that you mention in this book would kick the shit out of most touring bands. I know first-hand because I've performed with some, and I'll tell you they couldn't have gotten a job in Yasgur's Farm. The bands in our era were bad ass. The music appreciation level was so much higher than this generation of kids. People in general were very appreciative of good music and would go out on a Monday, Tuesday, or Wednesday night to see a band. I remember leaving clubs at two and three in the morning, and there was traffic on the road. It was like 5 o'clock rush hour.

Then one day it was like someone pulled the rug out from under us. The drinking age went up, and it was over. Not completely for Yasgur's Farm, but it wasn't the same. We're still playing a few clubs and doing some concerts under the stars. I'm proud to say that three members of our band have been with me for 20 years or more. The band still remains ferocious!

DANNY MURO
ROCK GROUP "WHITE TIGER"
INTERVIEW BY DAN LORENZ0

If you were a young man who happened to be a musician in the late 70s in New Jersey, you'd hope to eventually form or join a band. Naturally you'd have a dream to have your band become popular. If you had particularly big dreams, you'd fantasize about becoming as popular as the band White Tiger. White

Tiger guitarist Danny Muro lived that dream when his band moved up from New Orleans to New Jersey.

"New Orleans was a great music town, but there wasn't any way to make a living playing music," Muro told me. "You could play on the weekends, you could make some good money, but there just weren't that many venues to play. The club circuit up here [in New Jersey] was prolific. Lots of clubs. Lots of kids in clubs going to see rock bands. There were rooms everywhere across the whole Tri-State area. They were open every night of the week. If you were good, you could make a really good living."

How good?

"The club scene for us was bigger than it was for most of the other bands," Danny continued. "It was us and Twisted Sister, Zebra, and maybe Rat Race Choir. We were doing serious numbers at the door. Like on a Tuesday night we could do 1,200 people at the door at Mother's. You're talking about not having any money problems at all. Ever. It's interesting because it was much easier to live comfortably then. If you were in a band you usually shared a really large house that you could rent with a couple of the other guys in the band. The rents were like $500 a month for a big house, and you're splitting that with two other guys so your share of rent was now less than $200 a month, and your band could be grossing $12,000 to $15,000 a week or more. It was ridiculous."

If you weren't fortunate enough to experience this era in the New Jersey club scene it would be hard to envision the enormity of it all. As lofty a goal of becoming a band like White Tiger appeared to be... it also seemed attainable. This wasn't Led Zeppelin playing Madison Square Garden. This was White Tiger playing cover songs at Circus-Circus. Why couldn't you put together a band and do something similar? These guys were put on a pedestal, but somehow simultaneously within reach. One could dream. I asked Danny for any particular memories of Circus-Circus.

"We got a couple of great videos from that room. There was a guy who used to come and shoot videos of us, and there were a few really good videos. I don't even know where they are anymore. They were shot back then, and I thought they were terrific. The room sounded good. It was in a really good area. A lot of people came to that room to see us play. It was always, always crowded, and it was a lot of fun playing that room, because it was a little more intimate than some of the others. The people could get really close to the stage. It was a great room."

I had to ask Danny what it was like to be in such a popular band with regard to any particular favors procured from women. Danny just laughed. "With a band like us the whole event was magical. It was magical for us; it was magical for the audience. That was the goal when I put the band together and coordinated the talent within the band. Everybody was pretty much on the same page with what we wanted to create. We enjoyed big rock shows that took us someplace else. When you'd go see Jethro Tull or Led Zeppelin you'd escape. We wanted to be able to do that to people who came to see us. Everybody in the band could be bigger than life. We were very comfortable on stage. When that happens, you get a lot of the opposite sex wanting to engage. I think it's natural to have that kind of a thing happen...and who's going to say no?"

Unlike Twisted Sister, White Tiger never got a record deal. Today, Danny works at Fast Forward Unlimited. "We do big website design. We do commercial photography, video work, and graphic design," he shared. White Tiger was the proverbial big fish in a small pond...but perhaps one of the biggest fish to wash up on the Jersey Shore.

JOHNNY SING
ROCK GROUP "CONDOR"

Yes, it was indeed our own rock and roll invasion, much like it was in Liverpool... There were hearts broken, and love found, and dreams lost. But people found a place to go to be themselves, even if it was just for a few hours.

Johnny Sing is an easy name to remember, particularly when it refers to a singer in a popular rock band.

Condor was a big influence on every band member throughout our lives and still today. I never wanted to be the front man for the group, but when I got on stage, I was a different person. Nothing can replace the adrenalin rush we had five nights a week. People don't realize it, but when the Beatles came over here in the 60s, they played the same circuit as we did...they just happened to be in Liverpool, and we were in Jersey and New York.

When they came to the US they were polished. Over here, if you were an A band you played at the best clubs. If you were a B band, maybe you played a little. If you were a C band, forget it!

Any diva rock star stories?

It was like being a rock and roll star on a local level, and we lived life like it was our last day. It was so long ago, so I'll tell you now. We were doing lines in that basement from here to fucking Staten Island and somehow we lived through it.

What about the women, Johnny?

A large women contingency followed us around, but it didn't start that way. It was actually the guys that were following us and then the girls came.

How did you break into the competitive New Jersey club circuit?

Our break came when a booking agent, Steve Finelli, landed us a two-night gig that turned into three at 'The Cuss from Hoe' in Paramus. We were supposed to play just Friday and Saturday nights, but the place was so packed that the owner asked if we wanted to play Sunday night as well. He warned us, though, that Sunday nights were slow and not to expect very many people. I swear that the same ladies that were parked in front of the stage Friday and Saturday nights were in the same spot on Sunday night. It was all up from there. We went on to play 'The Soap Factory,' Circus-Circus, and the rest of the A clubs. From there we made our move to Staten Island, New York where our original music was well received.

Any Circus-Circus memories?

It was The Stone Pony of the North! I remember it was so packed one night that the bouncers had to walk us out the basement, into the parking lot, and up the fire escape, just to get us onto the stage.

Another memorable time for us was when we played at 'The Meadowlands' in New Jersey with Steve Van Zant. It was so cool. He was up on stage with us and everyone knew he was the guitarist for Bruce Springsteen. After my relationship grew with Steve, he went on to produce Condor doing original music. He was trying to mold us into an original band altogether.

What's going on in your life now?

I'm still rocking it with my band, 'The Rizing' in Florida with former Condor great, (Seaside Steve) Scerenscko, and other fine musicians. However, my full time gig is selling real estate in the Brevard County, Florida area.

(SEASIDE)STEVE SCERENSCKO
*ROCK GROUP "**CONDOR**"*

If you told me 10 years ago I'd be a private chef for a billionaire real estate developer in Florida cooking for his celebrity friends such as Bruce Willis, Uma Thurman, Jerry Seinfeld, and the governator Arnold Schwarzenegger, I'd have to say you were crazy!

From Florida to Beverly Hills to the Hamptons and wherever the G4 Jet took us, I was there serving up food the best I knew how. After that gig, I went on working as a chef for a private and prestigious country club in Florida, where I practice the culinary arts today. Preparing food for people is like being in the entertainment business. It's like being on stage… preparing the meal…watching people eat. And, instead of clapping, they're telling you how good the food is.

Let's talk about your run with Condor and the club scene of yesteryear and then we'll have dessert.

It was an amazing ride back then with the bands, the fans, the clubs, and the female groupies waiting outside the dressing room with gifts, party goods, and their apartment keys!" he laughed. "When I try to tell people down here in Florida about the music scene in New

Jersey in the 80s, and how many people came out to see bands seven nights a week and stood in line to get in the local clubs, they think I'm bullshitting.

One of the things on my bucket list would be to have Condor get back together for a reunion show. Over the years I've continued my career in music performing with Sam Moore of Sam and Dave, members of the Miami Sound Machine, members of K.C. and The Sunshine Band, and several others. There was a time I left Condor and started my own band called Top Cat, during the rockabilly craze.

Many of the members of my favorite Jersey bands live down here in south Florida now where I'm situated. Before he died, Clarence Clemons of the E Street band lived about a half hour from me, and my band down here was often a replacement for his band whenever he was on tour with Bruce Springsteen. Tico Torres from Bon Jovi is about 20 minutes from me.

JOE DOLAN
ROCK GROUP "**PROTÉGÉ**"

Joe Dolan is a successful tax attorney, specializing in estate planning in suburban New Jersey. Joe took some time away from his busy law practice to reminisce about his days performing in a popular band and his run in the competitive Tri-State rock scene. Joe was 21 and still in college. He played bass with Protégé, one of the most popular cover bands to ever hold down the stage at Circus-Circus.

We were like most bands back then. We started out playing audition nights, high school dances, proms, and frat parties at Rutgers, Stevens Tech, Princeton, and other colleges all over the area. We were willing to do anything to get our name out there and break into the club scene. It was very competitive, and there were dozens of bands like us doing the same type of things playing the same circuit. There were several versions of the band, but we got our big break when we recruited a new keyboard player and a great female lead singer with dynamic stage presence named Sandi.

After Sandi joined the band, we retooled our set list and landed an audition at Circus-Circus in Bergenfield. After auditioning, we were immediately hired, and within a few weeks we were packing the house every Thursday night. By the time we came on stage for the first set, the place was already packed wall-to-wall. The bouncers had to escort us and clear a path for us to get through the crowd to the stage. It was perfect, and we had that schedule every week for a year. We played a lot of 'all you can drink' nights and a lot of bikini contests.

The first sets were just a warm-up. The kids were ready to dance; they were ready to hear loud music. That first set would go by quickly. It was usually the second set that really rocked. By the third set, the crowd was hammered, and it could get pretty ugly!

I remember one night there were these two huge guys—each had to be 6'6"—out on the dance floor, slam dancing in the mosh pit. Just banging, banging, slamming into each other and knocking everyone else out of the way. I thought that was crazy enough until one of them chug-a-lugged his drink, raised the empty glass in the air. He then proceeded to eat the entire glass! The other guy saw what his buddy did, so he ate his glass too! Then, they went right back slam dancing as if nothing had happened.

And then there was a night in the fall of 1982.

During the summer, my brothers, a couple of my cousins, and some friends of mine would be in the audience at The Circus every Thursday night. Then, one night a guy ran over to me after we finished our second set. It turned out to be a guy from my town called 'Mad Dog' Davis. He rushed over to me and started shouting, 'Hey Joey Dolan, I can't believe that was you! You guys are great, man! It's great to see that someone from town made it! I'm going to be here every Thursday night. I am going to tell everybody back home and bring them down here to see you guys!'

Somewhere in the middle of the third set, however, a big fight broke out. There was a huge pile of people in the middle of the dance floor in an all-out brawl. It got so bad we had to stop playing. The fight was so big that we were trapped on the stage. After we stopped playing, I saw Mad Dog jump into the pile. He wasn't fighting, he was trying to *break it up and separate people. As soon as Mad Dog started to try to break it up, all the bouncers ran over. Unfortunately, Mad Dog was the first guy they grabbed. I watched as they picked Mad Dog up and threw him out down a flight of stairs into the parking lot. He literally flew in the air down the flight of stairs. And that was the last time I ever saw Mad Dog Davis.*

By the summer of 1983, the band was moving on. They left The Circus on good terms, with dreams of a real recording contract in their heads.

We were no different than any other band and had our share of internal fighting. Sandi left the group and we ultimately had to replace her. But by then, the legal drinking age in New Jersey had been raised to 21, and things kind of fell apart.

Joe knew that he only had a few more years of college and needed to get his act together in order to graduate. He retired from the music business in early 1984. During his own rock and roll heyday, he still managed to earn a law degree from Seton Hall University.

I was dead serious, and 100% committed to making it as a musician. When we had success, I was young enough and foolish enough to believe that it was going to happen that we would get a record contract and be on MTV. But, fortunately, I was also a pretty serious, hardworking student back then, just in case I didn't make it.

The only cases he loads these days are legal ones, and he has not played seriously in many years. But, he remembers his days under the big top fondly. *It was a great life, a really great and unique experience. I played all over New York and New Jersey, in front of hundreds of people at a time. When we played to a full house at The Circus, the stage and the entire floor of the building would be bouncing and swaying. It's an awesome feeling when you're on stage playing and singing to a packed house of hundreds of people who you don't know and everyone is totally into it. I was a college student by day and a rock star at night.*

There is success, and there's success. It's wherever you find it, and it's whatever truly makes you happy, whether it's a courtroom, office, or stage. Joe Dolan found it in those magical summers at Circus- Circus, and he's doing just fine.

AN INTERVIEW with MEMBERS OF THE ROCK GROUP "**THE BADLANDS BAND**"

Call them Badlands, The Bad Land Band, The Badlands Band, or whatever you want, but don't call them slouches. According to some of their fun-loving, beer-guzzling, and loyal groupies with whom I spoke, they could play Lynard Skynyrd as well as that famous southern rock group from Jacksonville, Florida.

With the exception of some original songs injected into a set, they covered other greats such as Molly Hatchet, The Charley Daniels Band, and a host of others.

On a cold winter night in December, 2013, I sat with three members of The Bandlands Band, including front man Rich Gulya, bass guitarist and founder of the group Ed Piersanti, and their loyal road manager and sound man, Bill Sasse. They reminisced about their run in the local rock scene and where they are today as musicians.

Rich- *When we covered Skynyrd, our looks and sound were unintentionally almost identical. It wasn't planned that way, we just coincidentally had the same look and sound. "The Badlands Band was also one of the first bands out there to take bluegrass music, which is strictly an acoustic form of old time country and electrify it. We took 'traditional' bluegrass songs and turned them into our own style of kick-ass music, in much the same way that The Allman Brothers did with blues. Bluegrass was always a 'cult following' type of music, but when we added a full band and rocked it up, mainstream rock fans accepted it.*

Bill- *I remember when we opened for The Good Rats at Zaffy's in Piscataway, New Jersey. I'll never forget that as long as I live! We were polar opposites in what we played, yet our manager called us at the last* *minute to do the gig, and we couldn't say no. It was The Good Rats and their loyal following and then us, the shit-kicking, southern rock band and our loyal following.*

Rich- *We had heard that any band that opened for The Good Rats had a good chance of being booed off the stage. It was like we were being set up for failure. But instead, the opposite happened. We got an encore. That was our big break and a boost to our confidence. Now we felt, The Badlands Band was ready to conquer the world!*

Ed- *Our first manager was Steve and then Jimmy came along to manage us. He worked really hard for the band. Jimmy opened doors for us to play in other clubs in and around Long Island and at one point introduced us to someone at a record company.*

Rich- *The long story short, it didn't work out. They wanted us to be somebody and something we weren't. They wanted us to be this original group, which was great, but when they told me to lose the cowboy hat and puff up my hair, that was just too much.*

Our run as a popular local band lasted about four years, and then the drinking age went up, the clubs fell apart, and so did we. Our group, like so many others, starting taking less and less money just to keep playing, and then the end came, and we broke up.

However, their love of music never waned.

Rich- *With The Badlands Band, I was kind of the jack-of-all-trades musician. Besides my role as lead vocalist, I also played the banjo, guitar, and fiddle. Today, I'm still out there playing often, almost exclusively as a special addition to 'The Nerds,' which are a phenomenon in themselves. They call me Rich the Cowboy Guy! In addition, I also play with other bands as a freelance musician and do recording studio sessions. Our keyboard player, Bob Gardner, is currently a songwriter and piano teacher and has collaborated with me on several original songs. My album was produced by Bob called, 'Dance All Night and Party Country Style.' Although the album is being promoted as 'Rich Gulya,'*

I'm proud to say that all previous members of 'The Bandlands Band' are on the album.

Rich Verge, who was on lead guitar and vocals for our band, is currently playing out professionally in Aruba. 'The Badlands Band' drummer Jack Yocum, is the drummer for 'The Nerds.' Bass guitarist Ed Piersanti now performs professionally in various NJ shore bands and has played on several occasions with Bruce Springsteen. 'Bronco Bob' Carlucci on pedal steel and lead guitars for 'The Badlands Band is also playing out professionally in local bands in the Tri-State area.

We're still out there having fun! That will never change!

RICKY POPS
ROCK GROUP "FRIENDS"

It was the best experience in my life. To be out there performing six or seven nights a week and playing with such talented musicians, was a dream come true.

Friends had a fast and furious 8-year run, performing in clubs and venues with enormous capacities, including clubs such as Hammerheads, The Fountain Casino, Mother's, and other venues all over New Jersey, New York, Connecticut, Pennsylvania, Rhode Island, and all of the mid-Eastern states. They played colleges such as Penn State, Rutgers, FDU, Seton Hall, and too many others to mention.

Everybody's working for the weekend! That was our attitude toward our fans. We knew and recognized that they worked hard at their sometimes menial jobs all week, so we wanted to give them their money's worth at every performance. We were a high-energy, kick-ass rock 'n roll band with great singers and great musicians. We opened for The New Riders at The Fountain Casino, Steppenwolf at Circus-Circus, and countless other national recording artists. Bergenfield was my hometown so anytime we played The Circus, a lot of my friends would come to see us. We were billed as New Jersey's #1 Party Band. 'Paradise by the Dashboard Light' by Meatloaf always ignited the crowd. With Todd and Jeannie on vocals and the romantic theatrics perfectly choreographed, you felt you were seeing and hearing Meatloaf.

Rick started out playing the saxophone in elementary school and switched to drums as a freshman in high school. Almost immediately, he landed a spot in a band called The Chandells, and played at almost every high school and church in Bergen County. He even had a gig at the then-famous Palisades Amusement Park in New Jersey. After four years, they added a guitarist and changed their name to The Colony and started playing many premier venues all over Jersey and New York.

We were doing so well that we were performing five nights a week. This is while I was attending Fairleigh Dickinson University to earn my BA in music, which I received in 1972. Sometime after graduation, I got together with two brothers who I knew through my cousin, and the band 'Friends' was born. We started booking through The Jack Fisher agency and began attracting huge crowds in New York and New Jersey. CTA—Creative Talent Agency in New Rochelle, New York—signed us and opened a whole new market, landing us gigs in the A clubs such as Creation, The Stone Pony, The Soap Factory, Circus-Circus, Royal Manor, and any other A club you can name.

Rick spoke of the band's concerns performing in New York clubs during the hunt for the 'Son of Sam,' also known as the .44-caliber killer during the summer of '76. After killing six people and wounding seven others, David Berkowitz was finally caught in 1977, but not before terrorizing New York City for over a year and taunting police with letters promising more killings.

It was scary performing in clubs in New York. Just knowing that this guy was out there and killing at random, made us a little nervous, particularly because we were leaving clubs after our performance in the early morning hours. You couldn't pick up a newspaper or turn on a TV without the constant reminder that a killer was on the loose.

Friends had a great run, performing from 1973 until 1981. But the music didn't stop there for Rick.

In 1982, I joined the Marching Band staff at Bergenfield High School as the drumline writer and instructor and then eventually became the assistant marching band director. I moved on in 1986 and became the band director for the Park Ridge School District. After resurrecting a program from scratch, I'm proud to say today that our marching band has competed all over the world including Pearl Harbor, Hawaii; London, England; Quebec, Canada; Disneyland and Disney World; Giants Stadium; and countless other places."

Marc Muller
Rock Group "**Molly Cribb**"
INTERVIEW BY DAN LORENZO
Jersey Beat Down

For those of you who have never been to the Garden State and whose opinion of New Jersey is shaped from episodes of the *Sopranos* or other shows depicting the Jersey stereotype, here's a prime example of just that. Many New Jerseyans are well-mannered and polite despite what is often shown on television. Sometimes, though, the people in New Jersey are exactly as those stereotypes are portrayed.

In 1980, Marc Muller was a 19-year-old member of the band Molly Cribb. Molly Cribb began to build a large following in Jersey playing Southern Rock. Things were going great until the band was joined by some new members who decided Molly Cribb would be better off switching booking agents. Marc explained:

"The two new guys in the band suggested we leave one formidable agency for another. [That apparently didn't go over so well with the agent!] There I was tuning my guitar at a club in Hillsdale called The Body Shop and all of a sudden these guys wearing ski masks and holding crowbars jumped up onstage after sound check [before the club was open] and started smashing everything. They also went into the dressing room and put a few band members in the hospital. It was surreal. I recognized one of the attackers who wasn't wearing a ski mask. He had totally identifiable blonde hair. I recognized him as a bouncer from another club, one owned by the agent we were leaving. I rode along in a police car to look for the guy. We found him, and he was arrested. I'm not sure to this day, but I believe a couple of the guys did some jail time."

Despite this ugly incident, the best in New Jersey came out to support Molly Cribb in their time of need. "There was a benefit at The Hole In The Wall on Route 17. All the big bands of the day did a huge benefit for us. After that it really seemed to catapult us in popularity. We really did well after that."

Really well until the drinking age was raised from 18 to 21. "There hasn't been anything like that scene since the drinking age was raised. The bulk of our audience was underage. Before the change, huge numbers of people would go see bands because they could."

"I went up to Berklee (Boston) in, I think, 1981 when the drinking age changed. I remember coming back [to New Jersey] from a break and seeing all the clubs closed. Bands trucks were for sale, lighting rigs, equipment…everything. Before that we had our own truck, our own sound system, roadies, sound man, light man…it was a real traveling show." Raising the drinking age changed everything.

Marc went on to have an impressive career after Molly Cribb. He explained, "I worked for Mutt Lange as part of country pop star Shania Twain's band for 10 years. I'm on Bruce Springsteen's *Wrecking Ball* release. Right now I have a band called Dead on Live. I transcribed Grateful Dead records, and we do a note-for-note recreation of The Dead."

TOM COREA
ROCK GROUP "DR. JIMMY AND THE WHO SHOW"

Just when we thought our lives were somewhat exciting... we ran into Tom.

When I interviewed Tom, the former drummer of Dr. Jimmy, he sounded like a 6 year-old kid that just came back from Disney World and couldn't wait to tell his friends about the trip. It was a nonstop barrage of war stories.

It was the 'perfect storm' as far as entertainment went. The drinking age was right and the tail end of the baby boomers wanted to see live music and party. There were clubs on every corner, so how could we miss?

At Great Adventure, we played in front of 11,000 people and almost smoked our guitarist with a flash pod that went awry. At The Circus, Gary, our lead singer and I, jumped into the pit with 'The Chicago Knockers' and wrestled three gorgeous girls on stage. Everyone was yelling and screaming while 'Too Tall Tammy' was grabbing my nuts. We were at The Stone Pony in Asbury Park when Bruce showed up. At the Rock and Roll Café in Poughkeepsie, New York, Robin Williams came into our dressing room and told us to fuck The Who and play our own stuff. And then there was The Dirt Club in Bloomfield. It was absolutely fucking New Jersey. It was the savior of all places. USA was coming in to film bands. I worked camera on a cable show there.

We had our own niche. No one could quite do The Who like us except Rat Race Choir. They smoked is off the stage!

The bouncers at The Circus were always good to us. I remember one night someone threw a bottle on stage as Tommy was smashing the guitar and the strobe lights were in play. The flash pods are now going off, and the amplifier is about to blow up...all part of the show... when this guy starts with me. Words were exchanged. I went to kick him, and I went off my feet. One of the bouncers picked me up and said, 'You don't have to worry about that.' They grabbed this guy and threw him down the stairs, head first.

Like so many other bands, it all ended in late 1983, when the drinking age went up in New Jersey and most other states followed. However, Tom never lost interest as a musician.

After five years of fine memories with Dr. Jimmy, I continued my love of music performing in several bands, one being Bad Attitude, an original and cover band. We recorded a few tunes, and in 1997 signed a deal with Attack Records in Canada.

If you had to do it all over would you do anything differently?

Knowing what I know now? I would have run it like a business, rather than a party. You want to talk business? You talk to Jay Jay French from Twisted Sister. He knows how to run it as a business. He's brilliant at that. Dee is another excellent businessman.

In 2002, Tom opened his own recording studio, Babyfish-mouth Studio, and has performed and recorded songs that have played on televisions, radio, and used in advertisements.

DAN LORENZO
ROCK GROUP "HADES"
BY DAN LORENZO

There were three clubs I wanted... No scratch that. *Needed* to get my band Hades into in the early 80s: The Soap Factory, The Hole In The Wall, and Circus-Circus. For my guitar tech (Dan Garber) and I, Wednesday nights meant going to Bergenfield. It wasn't an occasional visit, it was a must. I remember some thin crowds for the band Dreamer (which featured future rock-star guitar virtuoso Vito Bratta who went on to join White Lion) and better crowds for TT Quick. At the time TT Quick performed at Circus-Circus, they were an AC/DC tribute band. They eventually started writing originals and signed with Megaforce's Johnny Z who had previously signed Metallica. TT Quick and my band Hades would cross paths in the near future, but this was before any of that.

The best, but also the scariest, show I've ever seen in my life was The Plasmatics at Circus-Circus. Wendy O. Williams and her band had just released the phenomenal *Coup de 'Etat* album. My buddy Garber and I were so there. Wall-to-wall people packed The Circus. The band hit the stage and just crushed. As their pyrotechnics exploded, they brought the roof down. Literally. Tiny fragments were everywhere, making it difficult for me to breathe...or was it just sheer exhilaration? Either way the memory of nights at Circus-Circus is permanently embedded in my mind.

The big day finally came. My band Hades performed Judas Priest and Iron Maiden covers at Circus-Circus. What a thrill.

A few years later, I'd be touring America and Europe with a different version of my band Hades and then later Non-Fiction. I would explain to the other guys in my bands how special those days were. With them being a few years younger than I was, I'm not sure they ever understood the magnitude of what we once had in the "old days."

I went on to release nearly 20 records (I mean CDs). After I couldn't find a quarter for a bagel after a Non-Fiction European tour in 1993, I landed a job at *Steppin' Out* magazine. The bible of...what's left of our club scene. I'm not sure there will ever be a time quite like that again. In a word, it was magic.

DON SIUDMAK
ROCK GROUP **"SSSTEELE"**
INTERVIEW BY DAN LORENZO

Many bands that performed original music used a club like The Circus at two junctures in their careers: on the way up the ladder of success or on the way down. Aerosmith was one of the most popular bands in America in the late 70s, and guitarist Joe Perry had performed at large arenas around the world with his band. As noted, The Joe Perry Project performed at The Circus not once, but twice in 1982. For Joe's second performance, local cover band SSSTEELE was tapped to open. The date was October 22, 1982.

SSSTEELE drummer Don Siudmak remembers, "We were all thrilled because just a couple of years earlier we were high school kids seeing him at Madison Square Garden with Aerosmith. Joe Perry comes in, and since the space we were both occupying was so cramped, he literally needed to brush up against me to get by. I was facing forward, which was awkward but funny. He said 'hello, excuse me' etc. and was very pleasant while rubbing past me from behind.

"We shared the dressing room with him and were told of his demands from the club: a brand new metal garbage can filled with ice and Budweiser. We were told by his crew he demanded this everywhere he performed. Jokes were made as to him thinking he was still playing arenas.

"Before we went on, I was amazed by the amount of hashish that was on the table and being smoked and the largest lines of coke I'd ever seen. Anyway, it was a big party, and we went out and performed a bunch of Accept, AC/DC, Led Zeppelin, and Scorpions covers and a few original tunes. The crowd was great. We were really tight that night.

"I was talking to a couple of Joe's band-mates before they went on, and they mentioned he was pissed off at the recent success of Aerosmith's new video Lightning Strikes, which garnered enough interest in Aerosmith again to get them back headlining the Meadowlands Arena while Joe was with us playing a club. Oh well.

"Again he was gracious, although you could tell he had a little chip on his shoulder...not toward anyone in particular, you see, but just at his circumstances it seemed. He was totally wasted from all the drugs and alcohol. He did something on stage that I'll never forget, which illustrates his feud and frustration with Tyler and company. At one point in the show Joe started to play "Dream On," but after a few bars he stopped abruptly and went up to the mic, and said 'Yeah right! No fuckin' way!'

Anyway I got to witness a little behind-the-scenes history of a rock legend and hang with a childhood idol, and I got paid for it. A very memorable night."

Joe Perry went on to rejoin Aerosmith and not only match, but perhaps surpass Aerosmith's first wave of success. Don is now the CEO of Hell's Kitchen Music in NYC making music for television and film.

JIM GARCIA
ROCK GROUP "THE NERDS"

Jim "Spaz" Garcia wasn't always a Nerd, but he's glad he became one. In a wide-ranging phone interview, he recalled the first band he'd ever played with named Prototype and the years that followed.

The line-up of talent back then was incredible...extraordinary! White Tiger, The Good Rats, Thorin Oak, Flossie, Friends, Phantom's Opera, Nines, The Moderns; one was better than the next. We learned so much from these guys. What to play, what not to play; how to read a crowd. We learned from the very best. Now, when people come up to me during a break and tell me how great we are, I think to myself, 'That's nice to hear, but they have no idea of the talent that was out there in the late 70s and early 80s, unless of course, they're older. We would be a pimple on some of their asses today. Also, keep in mind that you had to be able to play drunk, stoned, or whatever back then. It was a different time. It was such a scene back then. I remember going to Circus-Circus at least once a month. I saw a lot of great bands there. It seemed that there were great bands everywhere.

Jim began playing bass guitar when he was just 14 years old and performed in clubs at 16. Several bands later, The Nerds were born.

The Nerds came to be in 1985, about the same time bands began breaking up and clubs were closing their doors, mostly due to the increase in the drinking age. As a band, we needed to do something different if we wanted to play. At the suggestion of our manager, Steve Tarkanish, we changed the name of our band and called ourselves The Nerds. The concept was that we were going to be the anti-band. Let's dress like nerds and not worry about how cool we look, but just play. We didn't expect to last six months.

After 29 years and still going strong, The Nerds perform more than 200 shows a year with a lifetime count close to 5,000. According to Ask.com, that's more than twice the number of live performances by The Grateful Dead and almost four times the number by The Beatles. They've sold out venues as large and prestigious as Carnegie Hall and have performed in countless places all over the United States and Canada. They've shared a stage with Sheryl Crow, Train, Southside Johnny, Hootie and the Blowfish, The Go-Go's, and too many others to list.

Yes, this is a cover band we're talking about. Not just any cover band, but a phenomenon that even the rock 'n roll aficionados can't figure out.

How do you do it? How have The Nerds lasted so long?

What's most important is that we love what we do, and we can afford to do it. We still want to get up there and play, and we haven't lost sight of that. This is what we do for a living. It's good to be a Nerd!

What has changed over the years musically, socially, and economically?

Back then you had to be good, real good. As a guitarist if you couldn't play blues, forget it; you didn't have a job. You couldn't get away with playing three cords like some musicians today. I'm not knocking them; that's just the way it is. If you played in a band in Philadelphia, you had to be a monster of a player, and now there are no bands in Philly. Today you've got bands with pre-recorded tracts and technology that's replaced the keyboard player and others, along with the essence of rock 'n roll.

Socially, there's a cultural shift. With Facebook and all the interaction you can get in your living rooms, why go out when you can be in your feety pajamas and socialize in the comfort of your own home? When I was 20, I wanted to go out, hear great music, and be with people. It's all changed now. Nobody buys a record anymore. You hear a good song; you download it for a dollar on your iPod or figure out how to get it for free.

MARK TORNILLO
ROCK GROUP "**TT QUICK**"
INTERVIEW BY DAN LORENZO

The movie *Rock Star* featured Mark Wahlberg and Jennifer Aniston. It was loosely based on how the band Judas Priest replaced lead vocalist Rob Halford with an unknown singer from a Judas Priest tribute band. One of my personal favorites, out of all the bands I had seen perform at The Circus was the band TT Quick. TT Quick was led by front man Mark Tornillo. I remember the band performing primarily AC/DC songs. I also remember an amazing song called "Son of a Bitch" that I had never heard before. The song was by the German band Accept. TT Quick eventually released a few highly regarded albums of originals, and many years later Mark Tornillo landed the job as the singer for...drum roll...Accept.

I got ahold of Mark after an Accept world tour. He had asked me to call him any day after 3 pm. I wondered if this was because he slept that late, considering that the last few years have been filled with recording and touring with Accept. Not quite. Mark still works when he's not touring.

"I'm a union electrician. Dude, I want my benefits and my pension! Three more years, I can retire with full benefits. I can do all the rock and roll I want," he told me. I asked Mark what he remembered about playing The Circus.

"I remember actually having a birthday party there, and I got a Budweiser cake. We did every Wednesday there for a while. What we used to do was call it The High Voltage Hour. We would do one set of all AC/DC. That started right after Bon Scott died. When we started TT Quick, it was as a cover band, but then little by little we started working in original songs. Then, once Dave Di Pietro joined the band...that was it. We always had a blast doing covers. We were working six nights a week. We had weeknights at The Soap Factory, at The Hole in the Wall, which was then Pebbles. I remember we'd play Ladies Night, and they used to make Mellon Balls. Trash cans full of Mellon Balls. You never saw so many drunken women in your entire life. Ladies drank for free," he laughed. "It was insane. The Soap Factory we'd play every Tuesday night. I'm pretty sure Circus-Circus was every Wednesday. There were so many good clubs up there back then. It was killer. The AC/DC thing worked well for us."

Mark is another protégé of the New Jersey bar scene who started playing covers. Years later, he is at the height of his career performing large concert venues and festivals with Accept in Europe and Russia, as well as mid-level size clubs in America.

BILLY MUELLER
ROCK GROUP "IMPACT"

The Flying Mueller Brothers, led by twin brothers Billy and C.J., and non-twin bro Donny, are rocking Jenkinson's in Point Pleasant Beach, NJ on this warm and sunny Sunday afternoon. Taking a break after a lively set, Billy is eager to reminisce about his days on South Washington Avenue.

It was different back then. There was this air of freedom! You could play music, and people would actually listen. You could jam for five or 10 minutes straight, and people would applaud you! It was more laid back, and you could play free style music.

We played seven nights a week with hardly a day off, and sometimes did a double on Sundays in the summer. It was a great time to be alive and a great time to be playing in a band. I told my nephew, who plays in a band himself, that he's not going to have the fun we had.

While it's easy and fun and not always accurate to imagine that our own generation was the "best" at any one thing, Billy's sentiments are common among the bands that played The Circus.

Suffice it to say, it was a different time. We were fueled by booze, weed and whatever else we could get our hands on, so the party just went on nonstop. When the clubs closed for the night, another party began at Sussex Street in Paterson, a home I shared with 30 or 35 people. We practically lived on top of one another.

The money was good back then. We supported a full road crew and five band members. We had our own box truck that drove from gig to gig.

The Circus was one of the best venues in New Jersey because it had a great stage. I remember the night we opened for Edgar Winter. We were told that wherever he plays, the opening act always gets the shit kicked out of them. I told the crowd that we're here to open for Edgar Winter, and the maestro would be out momentarily. No one booed, they actually liked us!

You had the right to drink at 18. Sorry if we wrecked it for the rest of the 18-year-olds in the country! Alcohol, drugs, or none of it, it was still a vibrant scene filled with music. We made it through those special times and walked away with memories that no one can take from us. Those days will never come back!

CJ (CARL) MUELLER
ROCK GROUP **"IMPACT"**

Circus-Circus was one of the most fantastic clubs! You guys had the national acts. The one I remember the most was Joe Perry from Aerosmith. He just had that fight with Steven Tyler and was going solo as The Joe Perry Project.

You mention national acts. Were there any others that come to mind?

I remember opening for The New Riders. They lit it up in more ways than one. The place was packed. We partied with those guys, and let me tell ya…no one could smoke more weed than The New Riders. They had the best sinsemilla in the world! Back then, it came from California.

And what do you remember most about Circus-Circus?

All the girls in that place…Oh my God! A lot of fun happened in the cellar and at the house we shared with several others. The road crew, the band, we all lived together. There was a constant stream of women coming through!

What clubs did you play at the Jersey shore?

We played regularly at Joe Pop's and Tides in Long Beach Island, New Jersey; the Chatterbox in Seaside Heights, New Jersey; Joey Harrison's Surf Club in Ortley Beach, New Jersey; and several others. There were so many, I can't even remember them all. The drinking age was 18 back then, and there were a ton of places to play. Wally's in Bergenfield, Mother's, The Soap Factory, The Hole in the Wall, and a million others.

What genre was Impact playing at the time?

We did a lot of Grateful Dead and had that whole following. I guess you could say it was jam music, but as the times changed, so did we, just to stay alive.

What other bands do you recall that played the club circuit?

White Tiger was great. They were a group of young, good-looking guys that did a lot of Led Zeppelin and other metal. Molly Cribb, Southern Cross, Condor, and a host of others were great as well.

Looking back, would you do anything different?

A lot less hallucinogenics. Just kidding! Well, maybe not! All kidding aside, it was big back then. Coke was the thing. Everything changes. We're older now. Everyone got married, had kids, and playing in a band isn't a full-time thing anymore. Back then, everyone was going for the golden ring, and unfortunately that didn't happen for us. But we did produce two albums. We did a rap over Mr. Ed, the famous talking horse on TV, and made it to 45 on the Billboard chart in 1985.

Riders for Rock Bands

Does the band Van Halen really demand M&M's minus the brown ones?

Let's explain that fabulously overblown rock legend right here and now. We went to our friends at Snopes.com, and this is what they had to say:

"The legendary 'no brown M&Ms' contract clause was indeed real, but the purported motivation for it was not. The M&M's provision was included in Van Halen's contracts not as an act of caprice, but because it served a practical purpose: to provide an easy way to determine whether the technical specifications of the contract had been read thoroughly and complied with.

Van Halen lead singer David Lee Roth told the tale in his 1997 autobiography, *Crazy from the Heat*:

"Van Halen was the first band to take huge productions into tertiary, third-level markets. We'd pull up with nine 18 wheeler trucks full of gear, where the standard was three trucks, max. And there were many, many technical errors whether it was the girders couldn't support the weight, or the flooring would sink in, or the doors weren't big enough to move the gear through.

The contract rider read like a version of the Chinese Yellow Pages because there was so much equipment and so many human beings to make it function.

"So, just as a little test, in the technical aspect of the rider, it would say "Article 148: There will be 15 amperage voltage sockets at 20-foot spaces, evenly, providing 19 amperes." This kind of thing.

"And article number 126, in the middle of nowhere, was: 'There will be no brown M&M's in the backstage area, upon pain of forfeiture of the show, with full compensation.'

"So when I would walk backstage, if I saw a brown M&M in that bowl…well, we would have to then line-check the entire production. Guaranteed you're going to arrive at a technical error. They didn't read the contract. Guaranteed you'd run into a problem. Sometimes it would threaten to just destroy the whole show. Something like, literally, life-threatening."

Nonetheless, the media ran exaggerated and inaccurate accounts of Van Halen's using violations of the "no brown M&Ms" clause as justification for engaging in childish, destructive behavior.

David Lee Roth's version of *the one documented show* where they were accused of M&M revolt was different:

"The folks in Pueblo, Colorado, at the university, took the contract rather kinda casually. They had one of these new rubberized bouncy basketball floorings in their arena. They hadn't read the contract, and weren't sure, really, about the *weight* of this production; this thing weighed like the business end of a 747.

"I came backstage. I found some brown M&M's. I went into full Shakespearean '*What* is this before me?'...you know, with the skull in one hand...and promptly trashed the dressing room. Dumped the buffet, kicked a hole in the door, $12,000 dollars worth of fun. The staging sank through their floor. They didn't bother to look at the weight requirements or anything, and (it all) sank through their new flooring and did $80,000 dollars' worth of damage to the arena floor. The whole thing had to be replaced.

"It came out in the press that I discovered brown M&M's and did $85,000 dollars' worth of damage to the backstage area. Well, who am I to get in the way of a good rumor?"

Suffice it to say, if you've got rock star power you can ask for—and get—almost anything. Were cocaine and marijuana not illegal, I'm sure it would've been in many a rider.

Besides other weird requests such as shepherd's pie (a weird mashed potato-topped English concoction), rainbow-colored condoms, a new toilet seat, six packs of Marlboro lights, 74 towels, underwear, and Flintstone vitamins, there were actual serious demands such as technical requirements that could make or break a show, as we learned from The Ramones concert when the power blew. There's security, stage, sound and lighting, dressing room, and a list of other important requirements.

My brother Jack was responsible for it all. This was his world for five years—every day, every night, and usually into the early morning hours. He had the knack for booking bands that were popular and could draw crowds and made them happy to play at our relatively small venue. Many of the acts he booked wouldn't normally play in a club that held only six or seven hundred people like our club.

Jack gave us the reputation of being not just a rock club but also a club that could deliver original recording artists, in a setup close enough for fans to be spit on by a band like Wendy O. Williams and the Plasmatics!

Originally, Jack worked with a promoter who was the go-between guys for booking national talent. After he learned the ropes, he was soon booking acts directly with the management of the different artists.

Still, I can't believe some of the contract riders that we signed. We once had a cover band that was making their first appearance at The Circus, and it was a total flop. We were paying the group $2,500, and only about 50 people showed up at $5 a head. Do the math.

Then, one evening, in late 1983, when we were barely scraping together enough bucks just to pay the rent, I was walking around the club, chewing off my nails, smoking cigarette after cigarette, and mulling over our latest financial loss. At that moment, the band's manager walked up to me and my father at the door and asked why they didn't have fruit in the dressing room, as specified in their contract rider.

I went to get Jack. This was his territory.

Okay, here comes Jack.

When the manager began to whine about the lack of fruit in the dressing room, my brother put his hand on his own crotch and spat out, "Here's your fruit!"

We had already spent thousands on the radio promoting the gig, we had lost a ton at the gate, and this guy was looking for fruit?

Yeah, fruit this!

So, we had our share of diva managers, bands, artists, and rider demands. Take a look at a few samples:

air-conditioned, ventilated and lighted. This room shall be in easy
ess to clean lavatories which are supplied with soap, toilet tissue and
owels. These lavatories shall be closed to the general public. Purchaser
shall be solely responsible for the security of items in the dressing area and
shall keep all unauthorized persons from entering said area by stationing a
representative of the Purchaser outside of the dressing room before, during and
after the performance.

B) Purchaser to provide 1 guitar tuning room.

C) Purchaser to provide the following for the Artist's dressing room:

15 Clean bath size towels
1 Full length mirror
4 Cases of beer (2 Budwieser, 1 Heineken and 1 case Lite or equivelant)
2 Cases of quality soda assorted (Coke, Pepsi, Tab, Hires, Fanta, etc.)
5 Quarts of Perrier
1 Quart of Orange Juice
2 Quarts of Cranberry Juice
1 Deli Platter for 12
1 Cheese Platter (Cheddar, Brie, Boursin, Swiss, etc.)
1 Bottle Jack Daniels
1 Bottle Bacardi Light Rum
2 Gallons bottled Spring Water
1 Bottle of Johnny Walker Scotch
Sufficient hot coffee and tea with milk, sugar, honey and lemon.
Assorted cookies and soda crackers
M & M Candies (plain and peanut)

SUFFICIENT ICE TO KEEP ALL BEVERAGES COLD AND SEPERATE FROM ICE FOR DRINKS. HOT
AND COLD DRINKING CUPS (cold cups no smaller then 16 oz.)

PLEASE HAVE THE ABOVE READY 3 HOURS BEFORE SHOW TIME AND SOME BEVERAGES AT SOU
CHECK. SNACK AND BEVERAGES TO BE PROVIDED AT LOAD-IN.

Crew meals for 12 after sound check (No spaghetti or Fast Foods).
After the show hot appetizers for 8 in band dressing room.
Assorted condiments and eating utensils.

D) 1 runner with vehicle is to be provided from time of load in through
performance.

E) 20 complimentary tickets in prime locations are to be provided by Purchaser
at no cost to Artist. Tickets shall be issued at the instruction of Artist's
road manager.

10) SECURITY

A) The purchaser shall guarantee adequate security at all times to insure the
safety of the Artist's personnel, instruments, costumes and personal property
from beginning of load-in to completion of load out.

B) All backstage security personnel shall be under the sole direction of
Producer's road manager. Please note backstage area is NOT a rest area for
security personnel on break.

C) 1 security person is to be stationed at the sound console and also 1 at the
lighting console from the time the House opens until the House is empty.

BEER, JUICE AND SODA: Two (2) cases Budweiser
One (1) case Miller Lite
Half (½) case Coca-Cola
Half (¼) case Canada Dry Ginger Ale
Half (½) gallon fresh orange juice
One (1) quart cranapple juice
Two (2) bottles Club Soda (not Perrier)
Three (3) gallon bottles Spring Water
One (1) quart Fresh Whole Milk (not low fat)

Hot tea and hot coffee, lemons and limes, cream and sugar
One jar of honey
Proper containers with ice (approximately 100 pounds)
to keep all drinks cold).

Fresh fruit in season
~~Fresh raw vegetable platter with dip~~
~~Cashew nuts~~
Sugar, salt, pepper, mustard, mayonnaise, knives, forks,
spoons, napkins, hot and cold cups and can openers, corkscrews etc.
five (5) Dannon Yogurts - assorted flavors
twelve (12) full size, solid color towels (not for the crew)
One (1) pound peanut M&M's (All Colors!)

Following   performance, the promoter shall provide assorted **fresh**
sandwiches (not packaged, please) for ten (10) people. These sandwiches shall
consist of Tuna Fish, Roast Beef, Turkey, Virginia Ham and Cheese and
Chicken Salad. Please no Salami, Bologna or rolled meats.

20 BREACH

In the event of any breach of the conditions set forth herein,   shall
have the right (without limiting any of the legal remedies considerable) to stop
or cancel the performance. The promoter shall be obligated still, to pay the full
contract price to STEVE FORBERT. Continuation of a performance, notwithstanding
a breach of this agreement, shall not constitute a waiver of any claim STEVE FORBERT
may have for damages or any other recourse which might be open.

ACCEPTED AND AGREED TO:

By: *Richard Bandopa*   By: _____
(PURCHASER)   (ARTIST)

DATE: 2/22/83   DATE: _____

5. Hospitality:

    A. Buyer shall provide a well-balanced, nutritious "hot" meal (no tuna please) for 4 to 6 people and shall be served immediately after sound check or by arrangement with road manager. This should include a soup, salad, protein rich entree and freshly cooked vegetables, (no canned, soggy shit please), dessert and appropriate beverages and related condiments. The health and happiness of musicians and crew will insure a successful performance.

    B. The following shall be placed in ██████ dressing room one hour prior to showtime:

- One-half case of imported beer (except Heineken)
- One-half case of assorted soda
- One-half gallon orange juice
- One quart apple juice
- Two large bottles of spring water
- One fifth Stolichnaya vodka (A MUST!!)
- Deli tray and assorted snacks (I.E. Assorted meats, cheeses, breads, fruit,)

    C. In Guest Room:

- One case domestic beer
- One case assorted soda
- Two large bottles of spring water
- ONE LARGE PLASTIC LINED TRASH CAN FILLED WITH ICE.

6. Ancillary:

    A. Artist shall have the sole right to sell T-shirts, jerseys, posters, pictures, programs, buttons or other souvenir items that bear likeness of artist. Buyer shall make space available for sale of above and may be reimbursed for providing a seller.

       Buyer shall to the best of his/her ability prevent the sale of bootleg souvenir items.

    B. No audio or video reproduction of performance shall be permitted without expressed written consent by artist or authorized representation. Any and all recording equipment will be confiscated at the performance.

If there are any questions concerning this rider or any aspect of Jorma's performance, kindly call

_____
BUYER'S SIGNATURE
RICHARD BANDAZIAN

1982

LIGHTING SYSTEM

24. In cases of club appearances, adequate club lighting to include a total of twelve (12) Fresnel and Leiko instruments with adequate dimming system.

25. In cases of concerts, a minimum of two (2) Luni or Geni trees with twelve (12) one thousand (1000) watt par sixty four (64) flood lamps per tree with twelve (12) channel electronic dimmer board are required.

DRESSING ROOMS

26. One (1) large, well-lit, and dry dressing room with private toilet facilities and electrical outlets capable of accommodating ten (10) people is required.

27. Dressing room should have:
    (A) One (1) full length mirror
    (B) Half dozen (6) towels
    (C) Soap and hot and cold running water
    (D) Ten (10) comfortable chairs

28. Dressing rooms are to be lockable with the key given to Artist and not accessible to the public.

HOSPITALITY

29. Purchaser will provide in dressing room, at not cost to Artist, at the time of sound check:

    (A) One (1) case of Heinekin Beer
    (B) Two (2) bottles of red wine ($5.00 to $10.00 per bottle)
    (C) Hot coffee, tea and condiments
    (D) If requested, a hot meal for Artist, which will be arranged in advance.

    (E) Pitcher of cold water with two cups on 18" stool on stage at time of Artist's show.

TRANSPORTAION

30. Purchaser will provide adequate transportation to and from airport and hotel when requested by Artist.

ACCEPTED AND AGREED: ACCEPTED AND AGREED:

_____   _____
PURCHASER   ARTIST

_____   _____
DATE   DATE

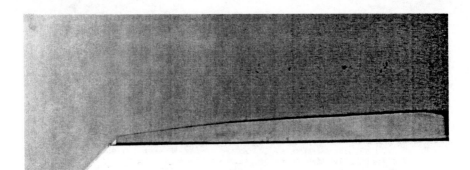

1. **BAND REFRESHMENTS:** To be placed in the artiste's dressing room 2 hours prior the the artiste going on stage.

12 bottles cold beer on ice, with openers.

6 boxes facial tissue paper

5 large bath towels

8 large bottles or cartons of pure, unsweetened orange juice on ice.

6 cans of Coca Cola on ice, with openers.

6 cans of 7Up, on ice.

6 gallons of spring water.

~~Hot tea and hot coffee.~~ *RB*

2 ten gallon waste baskets

50 12oz or 16oz cold cups

RB 50 ~~Hot cups for tea and coffee~~

Clean ice in a separate container for mixed drinks.

All necessary condiments, to include, openers, stirrers, napkins, honey, lemon juice, milk, sugar, soap.

2. **CREW REFRESHMENTS:** Tea, beer, soda and juice available for the road crew throughout the day, from load in to load out with all the necessary condiments, ie: hot/cold cups, milk, honey, lemon juice, sugar, stirrers, napkins, can and bottle openers, etc.

A hot meal for nine (9) crew members including trucker at 6.00pm after the soundcheck. (Not take away food.)

RB PIZZA

15. SOUND CHECK

█████████ requires a sound check of not less than one hour. During this period, the hall must be cleared of all excess persons not involved in the productions of the show. If the necessity arises, road manager may require that the doors be held for a reasonable amount of time for the completion of said sound check.

16. DRESSING ROOMS

Purchaser shall supply the Artist with two private dressing rooms. Both must contain a mirror, sufficient seats, electrical outlets, heating or air conditioning, access to private bathrooms and showers, a lock and a key which will be given to the tour manager, and adequate lighting.

In the event of no lock or key for any room, promoter shall provide a security guard to protect the privacy of these rooms. These rooms shall not be shared with any other acts on the show.

█████████ DRESSING ROOMS WILL BE OFF LIMITS TO ALL NON-TOUR PERSONNEL.

17. DRAPING

Entrances to the stage area must be draped so that the Artist can approach the stage without being seen. If the backstage or dressing room area is not separated from the building corridors used by the audience, the halls near the backstage area must be curtained off so that the crowd cannot get or see into the area.

18. CATERING -- CREW

Experience has shown that the load-in is usually performed with dispatch and increased enthusiasm if the crew is kept constantly refreshed throughout the afternoon.

Following the soundcheck, there will be a hot meal sufficient to feed at least 12 people. The meal will be served at one setting for all in a convenient location away from the Artist's dressing rooms. None of the food or the drink served at this time is to be confused in any way with the catering for the dressing rooms.

The hot meal must include an entree, fresh vegetables, salad, dessert and adequate refreshments.

All meal plans must be discussed with and approved by the tour manager, in advance of the show date.

19. CATERING - BAND

Purchaser shall provide the following food and drinks in the dressing room one hour prior to the Artist's scheduled performance and NO EARLIER. This food will not be shared with any other acts or show-related personnel. It is not related to any other food requirement throughout the day.

ALCOHOL: 1 qt (quart) Jack Daniels.

1 bottle red wine (Folinari, Soave, or equivalent).

Who's Bigger: The Band or the Club?

Did the band make the club, or did the club make the band? The answer depends on whether you were the club owner or the band. The top clubs were generally large-capacity venues that gave exposure to any band that played there.

It was cool for a band to say, "We're playing…" The Fountain Casino, or Creation, or The Stone Pony, Mother's, or any other brand name clubs. But we were the ones spending tens of thousands of dollars on advertising to promote not just our clubs, but the bands as well.

In fact, it was common for clubs to pay next to nothing for the opening band for a major recording artist. The band that opened for The New Riders, for example, got bragging rights and free publicity, and maybe some free drinks. For a lot of bands, the opportunity was enough.

Shortly before David Johansen was to perform at The Circus, my brother Jack got a call from Premier Talent, his booking agency. Would we let this pop/rockabilly band, Blue Angel, open for David?

Jack wasn't crazy about the idea, especially because the show was sold out, and we didn't need another customer to fill the club. But, he agreed to it anyway. It's never a good idea to turn down an agency as large and influential as Premier Talent. (Unless you don't want the next big act) It was always a hassle moving equipment on and off the stage in between large crowds.

So, the new unknown band was booked.

Meanwhile, down in the basement of the club, we've got two dressing rooms. One was nice, the other, well…at least one act called it a "shit hole."

Our main dressing room was like a living room. There was carpeting, two couches, a table for dining, drinking, drugs and a private door with a lock. The second dressing room was like a dark closet without a door. The only thing in it was a stained, ripped dark blue corduroy couch, an old wooden table with a Budweiser beer can acting as a fourth leg, and a cold, dirty cement floor. The ceiling usually leaked of coke syrup and other unknown liquids that dripped down from the bar above.

The room smelled like barf, piss, and stale cigarettes combined.

See where this is going?

So, it's almost time for the opening act to go on and of course, they've been awarded the terrible dressing room.

David Johansen is hanging out with the band and his friends in the main dressing room, relaxing and enjoying all the rock and roll accoutrements that come with being the headliner.

I'm in the kitchen, in my quiet place. I never sat in the office. The office was only good for counting money, making out checks, and sobering up. The kitchen was my space to think.

Here comes Jack to ask me something, when suddenly a petite, strawberry-blond windmill comes rushing up from the basement steps, nearly colliding with us. She's wearing tight spandex pants, a low-cut top resting on her thin shoulders, and hair tied into crazy pony tails, one headed north and the other headed east.

She must be in the opening band, I figured. No one else would be allowed downstairs without a backstage pass.

"Who's the manager here?" she spit out.

"That would be him," I said, pointing to my brother.

She fired with both barrels. "That dressing room is a hell hole, and why would anyone call that dump a dressing room?"

Jack, the Designated Prick, said, "Hey, no one came here to see you or Blue Angel, honey. They're here to see David Johansen. If you don't like it, you can get out of here right now."

I coolly slipped out of the kitchen and into the huge crowd, leaving the argument to the defense and the prosecution. Pushing my way through the crowds of people, I clawed my way from bar to bar to help the bartenders serve as many drinks as possible, as quickly as we could.

Of course, I'm drinking "one more for the house again," as we go.

Blue Angel was about to go on and the band lined up in the kitchen waiting for the security walk through the crowd and onto the stage. Their road manager calmly walked in, gave them a little pep talk, and then the green light went on. They made their way through the packed house and jumped onto the stage, about three feet off the ground.

Like a baseball pitcher warming up, they tuned, they tested this, tested that, and then the lead vocalist began to sing.

Every head turned to the stage as if spring-loaded. This voice was different—powerful, hot, and unique.

She moved like a cat running from a vacuum cleaner. Hopping here, running there, leaning this way and that way, always on the edge of falling down, and never missing a beat.

The spotlight followed her every move as she pranced up and down, kneeling and collapsing on the platform, and then hopping up again like a Jack-in-the-Box.

I was standing about 10 feet from center stage with the usual drink in my hand, taking in the show. Now, people were starting to ask who that lead singer was.

I didn't have a clue. All I knew was that she was incredible, and someone I'd never heard or seen before.

The band powered through their final song and finished their set, with the crowd screaming for an encore. Yeah, that's not gonna happen.

Still, I made my way to the soundboard and asked the guy working the sound and lights, "Who's that singer?"

"Her name is Cyndi Lauper," he said.

Who?

She, of course, became the soundtrack of your 80s, and her first album was your girlfriend's favorite.

That album, *She's so Unusual*, with "Time After Time," "She-Bop," and of course, "Girls Just Wanna Have Fun," hit the music world like a cyclone. She was adored, analyzed, criticized, and over-analyzed, as she re-defined musical, cultural, and fashion standards. It's not too far a reach to say she influenced not only every aspiring young singer, but also every retail clerk at the GAP, your young English teacher, and every teenage girl who was ever teased for being "unusual."

Her 1985 performance on USA for Africa's "We Are the World," will still give you chills. (Go ahead. Put it on. I'll be right here.)

For years after the dressing room incident, I said to my brother Jack, "Maybe, just maybe, she would have come back and played The Circus had you not treated her like that."

Thanks so much, Jack! Your karma account is officially overdrawn. Please watch for a notice in your spiritual mailbox. It's coming.

By the Numbers

I'll be honest. We made a lot of money back then, at least for a while. We served a lot of drinks, priced them fairly, and the people ordered. And they tipped. If everyone in the bar spent $7 on a crowded night, we carried a *lot* of bags of cash to the bank the next morning.

And everyone made money. The bartenders always had cash in their pockets, as did the waitresses. The Go-Go 80s were a time of spending money. Yellow-tied Wall Street investment bankers were playing the stock market like a cheap pinball machine with their mergers and acquisitions.

All around the world, nations starved. Ethiopia nearly starved itself off the map. But Americans rocked. And gave back. (Remember "USA for Africa"?)

Following the recession of the late 70s and early 80s, the American economy charted a steady uphill trajectory on its way to the boom years of the 1990s and the first Silicon Valley tech bubble.

Back on Washington Avenue in 1982, everyone was doing just fine. A college kid usually had seven bucks on him, and during the week, that would get them in to the club, along with a hot dog and a beer. As I said, the bartenders made money, the waitresses made money, and we made money. And yes, the bands made money. All of them.

How much did a rock band earn in the late 70s and early 80s? Here are the numbers calculated to 2014 dollars compared to 1980.

A good cover band could earn:

- Monday through Thursday or Sunday: $500 to $1,500 (today's dollars: $1,438 to $4,315)

- Friday or Saturday: $1,000 to $3,000 (today's dollars: $2,877 to $8,631)

Most tribute bands could earn:

- Monday through Thursday or Sunday: $750 to $2,000 (today's dollars: $2,157 to $5,754)
- Friday or Saturday: $2,000 to $3,500 (today's dollars: $5,754 to $10,069)

National talent (recording artists) could earn:

- Any night: $2,000 to $4,500 (today's dollars: $5,754 to $12,946)

Contracts for national recording artists and other popular tribute bands had several different arrangements. Here are some examples:

- A band could make $2,000, $2,500, $3,000, or $3,500, guaranteed, plus 100% of the gate (ticket sales) over the guarantee. The club made their profit at the bar, but in some rare cases the band could demand and receive a certain percentage of the bar income.
- There was also an arrangement that guaranteed a band $3,500 plus 50% of the gate over $3,500; the balance was split with the club.
- Or an artist could be guaranteed the first $2,000, the club the next $1,000, and the balance given to the artist or band.

Ticket prices were negotiable with the promoter. No one wanted to overcharge the customer and wind up with a small crowd or, conversely, charge so little that the artist felt ripped off. Concert tickets at Circus-Circus ranged from $5 to $7, about $14 to $20 in today's dollars.

The Bar Menu

BOTTLES ONLY

Budweiser $1.25

Michelob $1.50

Heineken $1.75

Coors $2.00

MIXED DRINKS

House-brand Mixed Drinks $1.25

Top Shelf $1.50

Long Island Iced Tea $1.75

Tom Collins $1.75

Alabama Slammer $1.75

All the other crazy shit $1.75
we could think of

Sabrett Hot Dog . . . . $.75
(the best meal on the block)

Who's got the Gun?

It's one thing to fill the club successfully every night, but it's quite another to empty it. It goes like this: As the band is about to end their last set of the night, DJ Tripp waits in the booth for the moment when he'll take over the music—his headphones are on, and his hand is on the record.

Another staffer heads to the coat room and gets ready to start the chaser lights and other special effects. This has to be timed just right. You can't just throw the house lights on and blind everyone. Although eventually we had to do this because not everyone wanted to leave. So, the DJ spins a song or two depending on the time and the size of the crowd.

Five hundred people in the club required at least 30 minutes to allow them to finish their drinks and get out the door before the magic hour of 2 am or 3 am on Saturday. Just one customer in the club with a drink in their hand after closing time could cost us our license or a heavy fine. It wasn't unusual for us to literally yank a drink or beer from someone's hand. We didn't like to do it, but we had no choice.

On one particular night, it was 1:35 am, time to gently move the crowd out of the club and into the parking lot, where you never know what was going to happen. Bergenfield's Finest were usually parked outside the exit door watching for trouble as the patrons were leaving, especially on crowded nights.

Interestingly enough, it wasn't like the police waited for you to drive off and then arrested you for DWI. After all, it was the late 70s, early 80s we're talking about. Wanton and willful drunk driving seemed to be tolerated. You can't imagine that now? That's all right. Neither can I.

Back to the parking lot. What began as a skirmish in the club between two groups of guys early in the evening turned dangerous in the parking lot as people began to exit. The glaring, trash talking, pushing, and shoving became fists flying. It didn't seem to matter that a cop was sitting in a patrol car right outside the door.

Watching the melee, the two bouncers at the exit tried to break it up, but quickly realized that they needed help. One went to the top of the stairs to summon help, while the other stayed outside. Jack and I quickly realized there was a problem when we saw the commotion and bouncers scrambling to the exit.

We raced down the stairs and into the rear parking lot. We couldn't believe what we saw. One of the club goers was on the ground, struggling with a police officer, as people gathered to gawk. Instantly, sirens blared and police cruisers with lights flashing converged on the scene. The lone officer had obviously called for backup before exiting his patrol car.

There were now at least six or seven police cars from Bergenfield, and possibly other surrounding towns, filling the parking lot with officers. But by now the fight had ended and the guy foolish enough to take on the cop was in handcuffs.

You have to be pretty high, crazy, or both to be fighting with a cop. Three of the brawlers were arrested, handcuffed, and thrown into police cars quickly, while the other three disappeared into the night.

The stunned and visibly shaken police officer involved in the melee was now looking under parked cars and on the ground for something, possibly evidence, I thought. Other officers were doing the same. So what could be so important?

At that split second, a chill went through my body, and I said to my brother, "Holy shit, where's his gun? There's nothing in his holster! Don't even tell me he lost his gun".

The search for his service revolver went on into the early morning hours, into the next day, and the weeks that followed. Further investigation revealed the obvious—during the struggle, his gun became dislodged from the holster and someone ran off with it. I think any cop would tell you that the last thing he or she wants to happen in their career, besides shooting someone or being shot, is to lose their firearm.

But the idea of having a police officer's service revolver in a drawer in your house would be just as scary. You'd have to be truly stupid to put yourself in that spot.

Newspapers got the story, and it quickly turned into a nightmare. As Police Chief Gavin Blaine, a school friend of my father's, told him "That gun could wind up in a homicide, a robbery, or whatever." None of those would be good scenarios, and an aggressive city councilman or commissioner could get us closed down over this affair.

I don't remember all the details, but a plea was made in the local papers for the return of the weapon. For two, maybe three long weeks, the story and the search continued, until the gun anonymously re-appeared.

They say any publicity is good publicity. Whoever said that should be smacked down in a parking lot.

Cedar Grove Inn
30 Pompton Avenue
Cedar Grove, N.J. 07009

September 21, 1982

To All License Holders:

We have made progress in stopping the legislation that would raise the drinking age to 21. The battle is definitely not over. The only thing that we can say for certain is that if the vote were taken today it would be a lot closer than if the vote were taken in June.

We need you, your employees and your friends to continue to call your State Assembly people and present our side of this issue.

In general, the two items that hit the hardest are:

1. The passage of this legislation will not reduce the number of alcohol related accidents; in fact, the legislation might even increase the number of accidents because more young people will be driving to New York.

2. The impact on the economy would be devastating. Besides the loss of tax revenue, we estimate that the number of jobs lost would exceed 22,000.

These are but two important facts to bring up when talking to your assembly representatives.

Our next meeting will be held on September 27th at 7:30 p.m. at the Cedar Grove Inn. Please make every effort to attend and bring someone with you. We can beat this legislation if we all stick together.

Our previous meetings have been at the Beef & Ale which is now under renovation. We would like to move these meetings around and if you are interested in hosting one of our future meetings, please let me know.

Sincerely,

Jay Holland .

JH/lc

Last Call

"You can't be 20 on Sugar Mountain, though
you're thinking that you're leaving there too soon…"
—*Neil Young*

In 1934, the original Alcoholic Beverage Control Act stated that the legal age for purchase, possession, or consumption of any alcoholic beverage was 21 years of age.

Nearly 40 years later, with the escalation of the Vietnam War and the US Army draft, most states nudged the Legal Drinking Age down to 18, including New Jersey. (New York had been 18 since the repeal of prohibition.)

The argument very successfully was, "If I'm old enough to go to war and die for my country, why can't I have a beer?"

The drinking age was lowered to 18 in New Jersey in 1973, a year after I graduated high school, and remained 18 until 1980, at which time it went up to 19, followed by 1983 when it went back up to 21. (Legal drinking age has long been regulated by individual states. California, for example, has always been 21, for beer or hard alcohol.)

But MADD (Mothers Against Drunk Driving) teamed up with insurance companies and law enforcement to put an end to the 18-year-old drinkers. They proved that fatalities on the road and other serious injuries were reduced as the drinking age went up. The State of New York raised their drinking age from 18 to 19 in 1982. So, the writing was on the wall.

New York finally joined New Jersey and raised the drinking age to 21 in 1985. Now that I'm a parent and grandparent, 21 makes sense to me, but it didn't help our business back then.

We had opened a rock club based on having a built-in pool of 18-year-old customers all around us, from cities, towns, and local colleges. When the drinking age was nudged up about a year after our grand opening, we had a slight setback. But it was no big deal. We could make it up somewhere else. We had a decent lunch and dinner crowd, partly because we wanted to make the town happy by keeping the restaurant format. That way, we could say we were a "restaurant and nightclub," which took away some of the stigma of being the wild rock club we really were. The restaurant actually brought in some revenue as well, but it was no comparison to the action at the bars.

So, now it's 1982. We're in the middle of a deepening recession that no one had ever figured into the numbers, and the pressure is on to change the drinking age to 21. The bars and restaurants are fighting it every step of the way.

Although I never joined that fight, a legal drinking age of 21 would be devastating to our business.

In 1983, the drinking age was moved to 21 and the next year on July 17, 1984, the United States Congress passed the unprecedented National Minimum Drinking Age Act of 1984.

This was the beginning of the end for clubs. The usual crowd of 400 on a weekday turned into 75. Weekend business went from crowds of 500 and 600 to 150. Our six or seven night operation turned to four. Initially, the bands and their agents didn't want a cut in pay but realized soon enough that the money just wasn't there. They made a great effort to work with the club owners, but it was too late. Too late for everyone. It wouldn't have changed a thing. We were all on the same sinking ship.

The piles of cash that once rolled in for the bands, their handlers, and club owners were gone. Imagine a time when cover bands were drawing larger crowds than national recording artists and crowds were large enough to require security guards just to get them to the stage safely.

And then the tsunami came. Clubs folded like dominos and bands were selling their fancy box trucks and equipment. It was over as quickly as it started.

And then it was desperation time.

Have you ever been humbled before? I mean, really humbled? To keep the place going, our popular and somewhat famous rock club was now reduced to hosting sweet sixteen, bat mitzvah, bar mitzvah, and children's parties on Sunday afternoons. I mean, I had a fucking clown once ask me to help him carry his props into the club for a children's party he was performing that afternoon. Didn't he realize on that very same stage—where he was pulling rabbits out of a hat—only a few short years ago Joe Perry, Cyndi Lauper, John Kay and Steppenwolf, The Ramones, David Johansen, Johnny Thunders, Steve Forbert, and a long list of talent once graced that stage? Indeed, it was desperation time.

With clubs closing left and right, my thought was this: if we could hang in there for a while, we would be the only one remaining. We could carry on and even thrive.

But that thought quickly disappeared.

We began to scramble for life preservers, but there were none. It was a challenge just to make payroll. The only saving grace was the one thing that always stuck in my head from working years with my father. "A mouse with many holes has lots of ways to escape," he said. This made me wise in structuring the deal when we originally bought the club.

We had two mortgages from the previous owners, and I made sure they were both assumable, meaning a new buyer could come in and assume the debt from us—essentially take the debt off our hands. The lease was the same way—all a buyer had to do was take over the existing lease under the same terms and conditions. If it wasn't assumable, the landlord could have doubled the rent or given unattractive terms to a buyer, which would have made the place impossible to sell.

The original lease that we assumed was for 15 years at a very low rental price. The terms clearly stated that the lease was assumable to a "qualified buyer" and that the landlord "cannot unreasonably withhold" to a new buyer.

Guess who the landlords were? Attorneys. Two of them.

It turned out the new buyer had no experience, so the land-lord tried to get out of the lease by saying the buyer wasn't qual-ified. We naturally responded that we had no experience in the same business either when we assumed the lease in the first place.

After some back and forth between our attorney and the landlord, they finally allowed the assumption of the lease, and the deal finally went through. We owned the business but not the building.

Interestingly, the property owners were two practicing attor-ney brothers, Harvey and Don Sorkow. Their corporate name? "Hardon Incorporated." You can't make this stuff up, folks.

Years later, now-Judge Harvey Sorkow made national news by presiding over the famous Baby M trial, a custody case that tested a surrogacy agreement for the first time in a courtroom.

Harvey and Don were actually nice guys. At one point, they were trying to sell the building and offered it to us for a really good price, but we turned it down. In hindsight, we should have bought it. The building not only housed us with 5,000 square feet, but also had two or three retail stores and two apartments. I think we were offered the building at about $225,000 or $250,000. Ah well, hindsight wears glasses.

My father grew up during the depression and believed that nothing lasted forever. This is the reason he never left his full time job at the *Newark Star Ledger* as a photo engraver. That turned out to be a smart move. Where was he going to get a job now at almost 60 years old? He had an unheard of lifetime con-tract with the *Newspaper Union*. When we were crushing it seven nights a week, I often told him to quit his job and to stop burning the candle at both ends. At one point, we were offered double what we had paid for the place by a couple of wise guys from Cliffside Park, New Jersey. I said to my father and brother, "Why sell? We're making a shit load of money."

Before my father passed away this past spring, I spoke with him about the club days and his memory of certain events that transpired. He recalled the time a bouncer consulted with him about a foreign ID and asked him if it was okay to let the kid enter the club. The last name on the ID was Kenyatta, prompting my father to ask, "Isn't the President of Kenya, a Kenyatta?" The kid replied, "Yes sir, that's my grand-father" As it turned out, the grandson was studying at Fairleigh Dickinson University. (Maybe he saw our advertisement on his book cover?) My father went on to talk about the good times and very little about the bad, although there were plenty. And even though his memory of The Circus days were all but faded, he would still call me enthusiastically from time to time, and tell me that he ran into someone that was at the club or remembers the club. Now some 30 years later in a bar or some party somewhere, I'll hear the same thing. "Circus-Circus? Oh man, we partied there! I met my husband there! I got my ass kicked there!"

Yes you did my friend. And so did we.

"Cover charges during the week are almost becoming obsolete because the bigger clubs are forcing the others to do so to stay competitive," noted Rick Bandazian of Circus, Circus. Pictured are (l-r) Rick and Jack Bandazian

WHAT'S THERE NOW?

BY DAN LORENZO

No night club currently sits in the old location of The Circus in Bergenfield, NJ. The exact location is currently split between two restaurants, Chapala Grill and Bamboo Grill.

The closest active club that still remains on South Washington Ave. is Tommy Fox's. When I first entered Tommy Fox's 17 years ago to meet with its owners, Thomas "Tommy" O'Reilly and Gerry Fox, I was quite certain I had entered the old site of The Circus.

"Tommy Fox's was never Circus-Circus" Tommy told me. "But everybody comes in, and we'll actually have tables of people arguing that it *is* the old location. I'll explain to them it isn't, but so many people are so sure that it is. They'll say, 'I remember coming up the back stairs.' That's how iconic The Circus was. Even after all these years of us being here, we still have people coming in every few months or so that swear it was Circus-Circus."

Tommy Fox's first opened as a traditional Irish Pub and restaurant. They were so successful they expanded and added a stage where cover bands still perform to this day.

"People still like to come out to see a band," O'Reilly said. "People like to see music played live. There are a lot of different places that do DJs. To a certain extent, the market is over saturated. I think Bergenfield in itself has always kind of been considered a music town. A live music town. It's a little more difficult these days, because people don't spend as much money. Still to this day...good live music is still a draw."

REMEMBERING "WALLY'S"
BERGENFIELD

Owned and operated by George and Mark Lefkandinos

On a warm summer afternoon in 2013, my wife and I decided that we were going to see one of our favorite beach club bands, The Flying Mueller Brothers. The band was setting up and scheduled to perform at the Beachcomber Bar & Grill, on the boardwalk in Seaside Heights, New Jersey. We met our good friends Joe and Sandy at the packed club and began to pound down a few beers. We quickly got into the party mode. I walked to the stage to say hello to the guys in the band, which I had known from the Circus-Circus days when they were called Impact, and I began reminiscing about old times. CJ Mueller from the group turned and wanted to introduce me to someone.

He said, "Do you remember Mark? He used to own Wally's across the street from Circus-Circus." It was a shock to see him again after these years. I didn't think he'd be interested in seeing me, no less talking to me. After all, we were fierce competitors back then. I can still remember seeing Mark at the top of the entrance stairs to Circus-Circus peeking in, just to see what was going on. Many times he would come in and have a beer, but all along I knew he was there to do a head count. He paid the cover charge just like any other customer. I look back on that today and say, "How could I have done that?" What a prick I was.

Although Circus-Circus was double the legal capacity of Wally's and could bring in greater talent because of its mere size, we still fought like high school brawlers, or so it seemed at the time.

Meeting Mark for the first time in 34 years changed all that. Maybe the rivalry between us was just in my head. We had a great conversation that included a never-ending exchange of war stories. I mentioned to him that I was writing a book about Circus-Circus and that specific era and asked if he would do an interview. I wanted the reader to get a club owner's perspective other than mine on what it was like operating a place like Wally's back in the day.

Just as I hoped, Mark agreed to the interview and here's what he had to say about his run in the roaring club and music scene.

"Those were crazy times. We met a lot of great people and a lot of fabulous musicians. My brother George and I opened Wally's in 1979, when I was right out of high school. We purchased the bar from the Mayor of Bergenfield at that time, Wally Rosenberg, which was originally a liquor store in the front area and a bar in the rear. We changed it into more of a club-style bar with food and entertainment, but never planned on having a cover charge. That changed of course, when Circus-Circus opened, almost across the street. We felt the need to upgrade our entertainment to larger bands to try and compete," he explained.

"As young club owners with a new concept, we were faced with challenges from the town. There could be 300 people in Wally's and 600 across the street at Circus-Circus on any given night. That's 900 people in a one-block area. No wonder the town hired two additional full-time police officers. But as time went on, we grew and learned fast the importance of having a good relationship with the local government. In fact, many of the people who worked for us would later become police officers and even chief of police!"

I asked Mark about the bands that played at Wally's and to share a few of his war stories.

"We had lots of great bands, but The Nerds were always our biggest draw. (Our legal capacity was 325, but we did 845 paid with The Nerds on the night before Thanksgiving. Sssh!) Other bands like Impact, Dog Voices, Good Girls Don't, and local favorites like the Back to Earth Band, The Willies, and TK Walker always packed the house, as well," he said.

"For many years after, and even today, I run into people with their own stories of sex, drugs, and rock and roll right under my nose at Wally's," he revealed.

In a dark club? Who would have thought? What can you best remember about your years at Wally's, good and not so good?

"The worst memories were some of the fights that turned ugly, and so often over nothing more than a girl. But that's love and that's rock and roll. Though I worked there for 20 years of my life and loved almost every minute of it all, I would never recommend it to my sons," he said. "Owning a club means many, many hours of work, a host of problems, and never enjoying holidays or weekends with friends and family."

How did the increase in the drinking age to 21 affect your business?

"When the drinking age changed, we started focusing on the restaurant part of the business, and booked entertainment to cater to that particular age group. We had no choice. Actually, the restaurant did well for a long time and became the local place for great pub-style food."

When did it all end?

"We stayed in business several years longer than The Circus, but all in all, it was a great time in our lives. And then, of course, in the early 90s, Seattle grunge music developed, along with its stage diving and mosh pits. That was the end for me. I still always enjoyed the music side of the business, but when I got older, and all the new kids wanted that type of music, I knew it was time to walk away," he said.

"We sold Wally's in 1999, and I went to work for Houlihan's out of Kansas City. My brother George went into the real estate business and owns two offices. And yes, I'm still alive and still married to my high school sweetheart. We have two sons, 25 and 18 years old. I still play a little drums when asked, but like so many of us, I'm a very different guy these days."

All Aboard the Time Machine

Okay, it was that damn jacket—my old, white satin Circus-Circus jacket. Still in pristine condition in my closet, covered in the same plastic the dry cleaner's left it in more than 30 years ago. Attached to the dusty covering was a receipt for the cost of cleaning: $1.00.

For all those years, it hung there quietly, pushed aside by a mountain of business suits and the detritus of 30 years of living.

Not to get too literary about it, but I think it remained quiet, biding its time like some Dorian Grey painting, waiting for its moment when it would exact its revenge.

Yeah, it's a stretch, but you get it.

I carefully pulled it out of the plastic as though I was removing an expensive work of art, and I held it up high. The bright white satin and the red logo of Circus-Circus on the back, took me back to 1979 all over again.

I carefully put it on the same way you'd put on a new dress or a tuxedo for the senior prom. Wearing this piece of history brought it all back.

For years, my wife and I couldn't even talk about the place. It was like it never existed, except when I would talk to others, especially strangers.

My wife's heavy heart about the club was understandable—I was out of the house day and night for almost five years straight. It took a serious toll on our four-year-old marriage, and that toll is the reason I waited more than 30 years to write about it. But that jacket started calling out to me.

Only recently, I was in Atlantic City at a blackjack table and a Ramones song came on the sound system. I looked across the table to a 50-something wearing a blue Yankee's cap and said, "I used to own a club, and we had The Ramones play there."

"What club was that?" he asked.

"Circus-Circus," I replied.

Two of the five players at the table shouted, in unison, "Holy shit, you owned Circus-Circus? I was there!"

The war stories started to flow between blackjack hands. It was part of my life back then, and I couldn't get away from it even if I wanted to. It owned me, and I couldn't think of anything else. After all, when anyone ran into me what else was there to talk about? The Circus-Circus radio commercials played every major New York radio station, day in and day out. The Circus-Circus jingle was stuck in the heads of all those young rock fans that listened to WPLJ or WNEW.

It was, "Hey Rick, I hear your commercials all the time. Who's playing this week?"

Someone else would say, "I saw your commercial on 'The Uncle Floyd Show' with Rat Race Choir."

It had been intoxicating, and I had started to live the life of a rock star—out every night until 4 or 5 am, smoking three packs of smokes a day, always with a drink in my hand.

It became normal to see fights, blood, puke, coke, weed, and customers stumbling out the door night after night. It even seemed normal to have a coat check girl who not only checked the customers' coats, but their knives as well. I guess that was part of the attire, especially if you were there to see a country rock band. I still have a scar on my hand from a box cutter a biker used on me as I was trying to help the bouncers throw him out.

So, the jacket and I decided that this was the day I was going back to this place and time in my life—52 South Washington Avenue, Bergenfield, New Jersey. Let it bring whatever it would bring.

With the jacket on my back, I got into my car. It was a cool September morning, and I began driving to the old location.

I felt like an aging high school football player squeezed into his old uniform, forgetting for a moment that he's getting on in years. Those days on the field before a cheering crowd in a small town stadium are creeping further behind in life's rearview mirror.

I drove onto Routes 208 and 4 through Fair Lawn, then Paramus, and headed for the club as if I were on automatic pilot. Apprehension set in as I approached the Fairleigh Dickinson University exit. I had heard for years that the club had changed hands several times, so I really didn't know what to expect. All I knew was that I had to go back to that place and experience the drive just one more time. I had to see what it felt like to walk in without it being my entire life.

Just ahead of me on the road was the familiar sign. "Entering the town of Bergenfield." I don't know why, but I expected everything to look different. The school on the corner, the car wash, and the nearby apartment building were all still there.

I approached the rear of the building where Circus-Circus stood and looked up where the sign once hung. Just for a moment, I saw the Circus-Circus sign. Now there are two separate signs representing the two different businesses that occupy the space. I parked in the same spot. I approached the rear metal door, our former main entrance.

I gave a good pull on the steel handle and walked in only to find the same black metal stairs that held thousands of rock and roll fans each week. I gazed up to the second stair landing where another sign once hung. *Circus-Circus Rock 'N' Roll Emporium.*

I stood at the top of the stairs and entered the dimly light hallway that separated the businesses. The original 5,000 square-foot club was now divided into two stores, with both operations independent. I tried to open the first door I saw, but it was locked.

With nowhere to go except down the narrow hallway, I continued to walk and realized this was the same hallway that separated two huge rooms that opened onto each other when it was Circus-Circus.

It was quiet. Way too quiet and just a bit surreal. Ricardo Chavez, owner of the Mexican restaurant Chapala Grill, welcomed me and asked if I was there for lunch. I told him I was, then I took a seat alone at the bar to take it all in.

He poured me a glass of red wine while I feigned interest in his menu. As he promised to return to take my order, I took my focus off the food and began to stare right through the restaurant as my mind began to wander…

The place is rocking. They're three-deep at the bar, my father's at the door collecting money, and Darren, Scott, and Ronny are pouring drinks and opening beer bottles as fast as they can. The sticky copper-top bar is packed with spilled drinks and empty beer bottles with no time to clear them. My brother's behind the main bar taking stacks of $20s from the register to make room for more. Tommy, the beer runner, is struggling to make his way through the crowd as another bouncer helps him navigate his way to each of the bars. He's complaining about keeping the coolers filled with cold beer, because they're selling so fast. The ashtrays are filled with cigarettes, and the air is thick with blue/grey smoke.

Harry's yelling at people to move away from the front of his bar to make room for customers that want drinks. Condor is playing Cheap Trick's "I Want You to Want Me" and their lead singer, Johnny Sing, is playing the crowd like a violin. The dance floor is full, and the audience seems to move as one.

Tripp is in the DJ booth ready to spin a record as soon as they go on break. His punky, spiky-haired girlfriend, Robin, stands in the DJ booth with him looking over the crowd. Everyone's happy.

"Sir? Are you ready to order?"

Snapping out of my daydream, I took a deep breath and began to explain to Ricardo who I was and why I was there. He brightened and began to share war stories of his own, and of course, all the people who continue to bring up the club's name. He said people still playfully argue with him, insisting that Tommy Fox's, just a few doors down at 32 South Washington Avenue, was the old Circus-Circus location. Not so!

If he was sick of hearing that story, he didn't let on. A customer is a customer, and many of his, both new and old, were friends of The Circus. Bergenfield was the kind of town where no one ever leaves, so people simply continued to walk through the door as the years went on. Rock and roll or margaritas, the door still swings open.

I left the restaurant and headed for home, my head bursting with memories and ideas.

The biggest idea I hatched that afternoon?

"I should really write a book about all of this."

I blame the jacket.

"Don't it always seem to go that you don't know what you've got till it's gone…"

Joni Mitchell

SOURCES

Newspapers: *The Record*

Magazines: *The Aquarian Weekly*

Web Sites: Wikipedia.com, Ask.com, diapermates.com, 420dating.com, Meetaninmate.com, wealthymen.com, farmersonly.com, pounced.com, darwindating.com, uglybugball.com, statisticbrain.com, howstuffworks.com, zappos.com, google.com, snopes.com

^ *Hollander v. Swindells-Donovan*, 2010 WL 844588 (E.D.N.Y. 2010).

^ *Hollander v. Copacabana Nightclub*, 580 F.Supp.2d 335 (S.D.N.Y. 2008).

^ *Comiskey v. JFTJ Corp.*, 989 F.2d 1007 (8th Cir. 1983).

CPSIA information can be obtained at www.ICGtesting.com
Printed in the USA
BVOW04s1303210115

384262BV00011B/437/P